A Reluctant Hero

THE WALTER SOMMERS STORY

Rick Kelsheimer

ISBN: 9798541333565 (paperback)

In Memory of
Louise Sommers and Terry Fear

Also by Rick Kelsheimer

The Hanging of Betsey Reed
Wa-Ba-Shik-Ki
The Adventures of Wabash Jake
The Lost Slab
South Union
Paradise Lanes
The Dark Slab

www.rickkelsheimer.com

SARK Publishing

Forward

Walter Sommers has never considered himself to be a survivor of the Holocaust. "How could I be a survivor when I never spent a day in a concentration camp," he reasoned with a high school student from Indianapolis. "So many people suffered and died in the camps at the hands of the Nazis. It wouldn't be fair to compare myself with those people who suffered so much." This was Walter's standard reply during his many years as a docent and educator at CANDLES Holocaust Museum and Education Center in Terre Haute Indiana.

He pointed to his friend and CANDLES founder, Eva Mozes Kor, to prove his point. "Eva and her twin sister, Miriam, were taken from their mother's arms at Auschwitz and subjected to experimental torture from the Angel of Death, Josef Mengele. They were the real survivors of the Holocaust. I was one of the lucky ones who escaped from Germany before the door was closed."

I argued with Walter that historians consider the Holocaust to have commenced on the evening of November 9, 1938, a night known as Kristallnacht. On Kristallnacht, Walter helplessly watched as Nazi mobs looted Jewish businesses and destroyed synagogues all over the city of Hamburg. On that night, Walter's father was arrested and taken to the Buchenwald concentration camp. Walter also had a ticket for Buchenwald with his name on it. In Walter's case, however, he managed to stay one step ahead of the Nazi's. He was hidden by a Romanian family until the riots ended and things calmed down. Instead of leaving for South America on a freighter from Hamburg where he was working as an apprentice, Walter chose to go back home to save his family. He hid from the authorities long enough to make his way from Hamburg to his boyhood home in Frankfurt.

After two months of jumping through Nazi, British and American bureaucratic hoops and suffering the loss of ninety percent of the family's substantial wealth, Walter managed to orchestrate and obtain exit visas for himself, his parents and sister, Lore. In January of 1939, his family left Holland on a Dutch passenger ship for the United States. After six years as a Jewish teenager in Nazi Germany, Walter Sommers and his family got a fresh start in New York City.

As I tried to convince Walter that he was, indeed, a Holocaust survivor, I received a full dose of German stubbornness, which I had experienced first-hand with my own German grandfather. I was forced to accept the inevitable. Walter Sommers does not want to be known as a Holocaust Survivor. Since there is a short movie in existence titled: *Walter Sommers: A Kristallnacht Survivor*, I decided to use that moniker when referring to Walter.

I thought that suffering through six years of Nazi persecution and living to tell the story would be the defining moment of Walter's life. He was a German Jew who escaped from Adolf Hitler's Germany; thousands of books have been written on that very subject. Walter's experience with the Nazi's is riveting and is one that needs to be told, however, it wouldn't portray the entire story. Even though Walter Sommers was shaped by a youth spent under Hitler and the Nazi's, he didn't let one of the darkest periods in history define him.

In Walter Sommer's hundred years, he has been called a loyal German, a dirty Jew, a refugee, an immigrant, G.I. Joe, a liberator, an entrepreneur, a business man, a civil rights activist, a husband, a father, a grandfather, an educator, a philanthropist and last, but not least—a hero.

After retirement, Walter felt the need to give back to his adopted country. He spent his days as a volunteer for a number of organizations. In the late 1990s, at the request of Eva Kor, Walter became a docent at CANDLES. At that time he began to educate a new generation about the Holocaust. It didn't take long for people to realize that Walter Sommers was a living breathing encyclopedia, whose perspective on Germany and the Holocaust was unique. He was a German Jew who loved Germany, despite what the country had done to him and his family. He equally loved the United States and became a card-carrying member of what Tom Brokaw referred to as 'America's Greatest Generation.'

In the span of just a few years, Walter Sommers went from being a Jewish teenager living under Nazi rule, to a struggling immigrant in America, to a liberator of four Pacific Islands as a Corporal in the United States Army. He was preparing for the invasion of the Japanese mainland when the atomic bombs were dropped in Hiroshima and Nagasaki. After the Japanese surrendered, Walter served as part in the occupying force in Tokyo.

Walter experienced World War II from so many different and unique situations, it gave him a broader prospective of the conflict. He decided to teach about the story of Holocaust from his vantage point.

At age 99 Walter could still be heard explaining to students of all ages about how World War II and the Holocaust could have been prevented. By teaching the facts without bias, future atrocities can be avoided. It wouldn't be accurate to say Walter is not opinionated about what he teaches. He most definitely is. Within minutes of listening to his lecture, he will tell you about how The Treaty of Versailles was responsible for Hitler's rise to power. "If Germany had been treated fairly after World War I in the manner they were treated after World War II—Hitler would still be hanging wallpaper in Austria."

When a group of German Nationals visited CANDLES in 2015 they expected the worst when they heard hear Walter speak. "Go ahead and give us hell about what the Nazis did to the Jews, was the first thing they said to me," Walter explained. "I think they were used to having the modern-day Germans lumped into the same category as Hitler's Nazis." Walter assured them that wasn't his intention. He loved the Germany of his youth and despite the Holocaust, he never ceased to love his homeland. He despised what the Nazis did to the Jews and to Germany itself.

Eventually, Walter was able to forgive the Nazis, but he made it clear that their atrocities should never be forgotten. "The only way to keep the Holocaust from reoccurring is by accurately teaching how and why it happened. If we don't learn from our history, we are bound to repeat the same mistakes."

The Germans who listened that day were so impressed by Walter's message, that word reached Berlin. A few months later, Walter received a phone call from the German Consul General informing him that German President Joachim Gauck was awarding him the Cross of the Order of Merit of the Federal Republic of Germany. In recognition of his exceptional services in promoting peace and tolerance among peoples and cultures through Holocaust education. His first response was "Are you sure you have the right Walter Sommers?" They assured him he was.

At age 95, Walter Sommers received a standing ovation at CANDLES upon receiving the medal and shaking the hand of the German Consul General, Herbert Quell. Quell explained why Sommers was chosen for the award. "President Gauck has awarded you this high distinction for your outstanding contribution to German-American relations and better understanding. This life of volunteerism and reconciliation with your country of birth formed the basis for being chosen for the award."

Quell went on to say: "As a docent with the authority of your personal life experience, you have, for the past 20 years or so, engaged yourself in talking about Jewish history in Germany and Europe. You have promoted a realistic, non-defamatory image of my country. You have presented the long-standing commitment of the Federal Republic of Germany to become and to act as a reliable and responsible democracy, respecting and implementing human rights."

"Through your voluntary work of roughly two decades, you have reached many people who are interested in Germany. You have invested time and energy in telling people that beyond the 12 years of the Nazi terror regime, there lies a rich history in which Jews played an essential role."

"You have put present-day politics of Germany in context and contributed to the knowledge of my country," Quell said. "It seems that in this process, you also redefined your own relationship with Germany."

Walter's teachings are shaped by his personal journey. After receiving the Cross of the Order of Merit, Walter's thoughts traveled back to his to his paternal Grandfather, Isaac. Ironically, Isaac Sommer was awarded the same award 144 years earlier, was pinned onto Isaac Sommer's chest by William I, King of Prussia in 1871 for meritorious service in the Franco-Prussian war.

In a way, receiving the medal reconciled Walter with the pre-Hitler Germany of his youth. In 1939, Walter escaped the Nazi Reich with nothing but the clothes on his back. Seventy-six years later, his beloved Germany welcomed him back as a hero.

Walter at CANDLES

"Who would want to read a book about me?" Walter has asked several times during our visits over the past two years. "There are so many people who are much more deserving than me." Walter views himself as an ordinary man who simply did what he had to do to get by in life. In many ways, that statement is absolutely true. His life, however, has been anything but ordinary. Through circumstances beyond his control, Walter's journey has taken numerous twists and turns, his story unfolds like the plot of a novel. Walter was dealt several bad hands during his early years. Not only did he survive—he thrived. He saw every roadblock as an opportunity and then made the best of things. Walter's life story is one of an ordinary man who lived an extraordinary life. His front row seat to the good and the bad of the twentieth century is one of a kind.

This informal biography is intended to not only chronicle the amazing life of Walter Sommers, but to also present the unique perspective of his 100 years. Walter has a story of perseverance and a message of hope that should be preserved for generations to come.

Train ride to Frankfurt

November 15, 1938

THE TEMPERATURE WAS DROPPING BELOW freezing as the sun disappeared behind the massive clock tower of the Hamburg Hauptbahnhof Railway Station. Walter Sommer was trying to stay in the shadows while struggling with an over-sized suitcase as he pushed his bicycle across the brick-paved street. Dozens of men in Nazi uniforms were milling around the station which only added to his anxiety. There was an arrest warrant with his name on it, along with a ticket to a concentration camp if anyone learned that he was a Jew. With a light complexion, sandy brown hair and sky-blue eyes, Walter blended into the hustle and bustle of Hamburg. He tried to act inconspicuously as the Gestapo and SA Stormtroopers combed the train station in search of escaping Jews. He prayed that they didn't ask for his identity papers as he approached the ticket counter. Even though 'Sommer' was a common surname in Germany and wouldn't have identified Walter as a Jew, the giant red J stamped onto his papers most assuredly would.

Walter avoided making eye contact as he handed the cashier exact change for a ticket to Frankfurt on the evening express. The cashier never looked up and more importantly didn't ask for his papers. Walter hurried with his bicycle and suitcase to the baggage car where a pair of SS officers were standing on the platform. The Schutzstaffel, also known as the SS, was responsible for enforcing Nazi policies. Under Heinrich Himmler's leadership the SS became the most fanatical group in Germany's attempt to become a pure Aryan state. To attain membership all SS officer candidates had to provide proof of Aryan ancestry back to 1750. This ideology created a zealotry which was obsessed with persecuting Jews.

Hamburg Train Station

Walter hesitated at first but realized that any hesitation on his part would draw attention. If asked for his papers, he would immediately be arrested and sent to Buchenwald. He couldn't let that happen. His entire family was depending on him.

He took a deep breath and walked directly to the baggage car. Unfortunately, the bicycle was too heavy for him to lift into the car by himself. As he struggled, a line began to form behind him. The last thing he wanted to do was draw attention to himself, however that is exactly what he did. His heart began to race as he saw one of the SS officers walking toward him. Fearing the worst, he was relieved when the officer arrived with a smile on his face. "Let me help you with that," he said as he helped push the bike aboard.

Walter thanked him and hurried to find his seat in the front of the train keeping his head down as he passed through the coach cars which were filling with soldiers. There were dozens if not hundreds of Nazis on the train. It confirmed the wisdom of spending extra money for a first-class ticket. "I bought the ticket in the compartment car because I was afraid the open seating cars would be full of Nazis. And I was right," Walter explained.

"Since there were only six people per each compartment. I figured it would be much safer in first-class."

Breathing a sigh of relief when he found the compartment empty, Walter took a seat next to the window in hopes that he would be riding alone. Waiting in the compartment he passed the time by reading the rules of the train which were posted in German, French and Italian. Walter chuckled when he realized that one rule was written in Italian and not the two other languages: No Spitting on the Floor. "I don't know if it was true or not, but the Italians had a reputation for spitting."

His smile immediately disappeared when the compartment door opened, and five men claimed the remaining seats. Three of the men were brown shirted SA Storm Troopers. The other two had Swastika lapel pins. "They were some kind of Nazi Party workers," Walter explained. They greeted him politely and continued with their conversation. "I didn't ask them any personal questions and only spoke when they addressed me personally. I minded my own business and keep my mouth shut." As the Nazis conversed among themselves, Walter pulled down his cap and pretended to go to sleep. Unfortunately, sleep wasn't forthcoming as the events of the past few days replayed in his mind.

Walter had known for years that there was no future for him in Germany. Since 1933 when Hitler came to power, He had seen his citizenship revoked along with the right to go to college. Walter could see the writing on the wall and with the help of his father, secured an apprenticeship with Maass & Reige; an exporting company based in the Port of Hamburg which shipped German, French, and Czech goods to Central and South America.

Because of his private school education Walter was fluent in English, Spanish and French. This made him invaluable in making daily trips to foreign consulates carrying documents and invoices. His duties required him to type in German, Spanish and English. Walter also ran errands and made bank deposits which allowed him to move freely about the city. Despite the ever-closing Nazi grip there was a normalcy to Walter's day to day life. He rented a room from a retired teacher who required much to his chagrin, that Walter be in bed by eight o'clock. The rooming situation had been arranged by his father. Even though he was seventeen and living eight hours from Frankfurt, Walter still obeyed his father's rules.

Undeterred by the early curfew Walter often enjoyed the company of his Romanian girlfriend, Tea Jaegerman. Amazingly, the Jaegerman family had immigrated to Germany from Romania in 1934 because Germany had the reputation of treating their Jewish population well. "Before the Nazis came to power, nobody cared if you were Catholic, Lutheran or Jewish. We were all Germans and proud of it," Walter explained. "Jewish life in Germany was comparable to Jewish life in America today. We were productive members of society trying to get along as best we could. This was the case under the Weimar Republic, but when Adolf Hitler came to power in 1933 the opposite became the rule. After migrating to Germany the Jaegermans soon realized that they had traded one oppressor for another.

Tea's father was a furrier and encouraged the budding romance, hoping that things would go better for his daughter if she found a nice German boy to marry. In pre-Hitler Germany, Walter would have been seen as a German rather than Jewish. On the eve of Kristallnacht this no longer applied. After the Nuremberg Laws were instituted, German Jews were considered to be members of an inferior race. Ironically, Romanian Jews, like the Jaegerman family were viewed as Romanian and not Jewish because of Germany's non-aggression treaty with Romania.

Nuremberg Laws

Law for the Protection of German Blood and German Honor
Moved by the understanding that purity of German blood is the essential condition for the continued existence of the German people, and inspired by the inflexible determination to ensure the existence of the German nation for all time, the Reichstag has unanimously adopted the following law, which is promulgated herewith:

Article 1

1. Marriages between Jews and citizens of German or related blood are forbidden. Marriages nevertheless concluded are invalid, even if concluded abroad to circumvent this law.
2. Annulment proceedings can be initiated only by the state prosecutor.

Article 2

Extramarital relations between Jews and citizens of German or related blood are forbidden.

Article 3

Jews may not employ in their households female citizens of German or related blood who are under 45 years old.

Article 4

1. Jews are forbidden to fly the Reich or national flag or display Reich colors.
2. They are, on the other hand, permitted to display the Jewish colors. The exercise of this right is protected by the state.

Article 5

1. Any person who violates the prohibition under Article 1 will be punished with prison with hard labor.
2. A male who violates the prohibition under Article 2 will be punished with prison or prison with hard labor.
3. Any person violating the provisions under Articles 3 or 4 will be punished with prison with hard labor for up to one year and a fine, or with one or the other of these penalties.

Morning of Kristallnacht in Hamburg

On the morning of November 9, 1938, Walter rode his bicycle to Maass & Reige not knowing this would be the last week of his employment with the company. He waited at the designated street corner for his friend and fellow apprentice named Heinz. Despite the fact that Heinz was a member of the Hitler Youth, Walter and Heinz had become close friends. "He couldn't type and only spoke German, so I had to do all of the work that needed to be typewritten or translated from English and Spanish. He was a strong fellow and did most of the physical work, so we made a pretty good team," Walter remembered. "We peddled through the heavy downtown traffic and took the ferryboat across Outer Alster Lake. It was a beautiful sunny day." Everything seemed normal until they arrived at work. Herr Gottlieb, the company's owner, wasn't at his desk. Gottlieb, a German Jew who was married to a British Christian woman had fled to England on one of the company's freighters in the middle of the night. Someone had apparently warned him of the impending violence to be unleashed on the Jewish Population. Gottlieb left instructions for Walter to leave the office immediately and take inventories aboard one of the company's ocean-going freighters in port at the time. Gottlieb was afraid that the Nazis would arrest any and all adult Jewish men in a nationwide round-up and hoped was that Walter could avoid arrest by remaining out of sight during the dragnet. If things turned dire, Walter was instructed to leave on an outgoing ship to Argentina or Costa Rica. Gottlieb had promised Walter employment in any of Maass & Reige's South or Central American offices. With Walter fluent in Spanish, the transition would be fairly easy. Gottlieb's warning would turn out to be prophetic.

Walter always tried to look at every situation in a positive light. Instead of cowering before the Nazis, Walter went about his duties on November 9th as if nothing had happened. "I actually enjoyed the days working on ships. There was nothing I could do about what was going on outside, so I decided to do my job as best as I could," Walter explained. "The work was enjoyable as we did inventories."

Although nothing happened on the morning of the 9th there was a flurry of activity around Hamburg as the SA and Hitler Youth units prepared to unleash the violent pogrom against a largely unsuspecting Jewish population.

At quitting time Walter rode his bicycle toward home. "We were talking and laughing when we came upon a howling street mob consisting of some very rough and dirty people. Armed with sledgehammers and crowbars, they were destroying all downtown stores that had been marked at being Jewish-owned. While this was going on, the police stood by and did nothing. They were there to protect the Gentile-owned businesses only. There was shouting and screaming, and people were running away from the violence. The mob threw the merchandise into the streets and then ruined it with water, fire, and ink. The stores themselves were utterly destroyed. Jewish men were beaten, rounded up and taken to police stations where they were detained until transportation to a concentration camp could be arranged.

"It was devastating," Walter admitted, "but I really didn't know what was going on. Heinz had tears in his eyes." Walter started to worry that he might also be caught up in the violence, however because Heinz wore a Swastika lapel pin, the mob dismissed them as just two onlookers on their bicycles.

Walter and Heinz watched as men threw out everything they could lay their hands on; furniture; crystal; china; silver; clothes—even a piano. Everything was hurled through the second-floor windows to the approval of the crowd below.

As they continued toward home they came upon one of Hamburg's oldest synagogues. Another mob, consisting of Hitler Youth and brown-shirted para-military types had set the ancient building on fire while members of the Hamburg Fire Department stood by and watched. Some were throwing torches and Molotov cocktails into the synagogue while others heaved bricks and rocks through priceless stained-glass windows. Some of the firemen wanted to help but were kept at bay by SA Brownshirts. Just as with the downtown businesses, they were there to protect only the property owned by the non-Jews. Some of the temple's congregants risked their lives to save priceless Torahs and other artifacts from the flames. Some of them perished in the fire, while others were beaten and arrested and forced to watch as the sacred scrolls were burned in the streets. Amazingly, some of the Torahs were smuggled to safety.

Walter couldn't fathom what he was seeing. He knew things had been bad for Jews in Germany, but even with all of the Nazi anti-Semitic policies, he couldn't believe Germans were capable of this. Not the German people he had known all his life. Part of him had sensed this day was coming but witnessing the actual events of Kristallnacht seemed surreal and alien to his German sensibilities. "This was so wasteful and unnecessary," he thought. Gentiles and Jews had lived peacefully together in Germany for hundreds of years. His father and uncles had fought in the German Army during World War I. His grandfather had received the Iron Cross from Kaiser Wilhelm, himself. "We were good Germans and didn't deserve this." And yet it was happening right before his eyes. Walter's beloved Germany had declared war on its Jewish population.

Walter and Heinz watched helplessly as the synagogue burned. When they finally decided to leave, both boys had tears in their eyes. A line had been drawn in the sand and the two friends were on opposite sides. Heinz escorted Walter to his boarding house and then pedaled off into the night. Walter watched him and realized that the two friends were now committed to separate paths. Decades later, Walter would still lament the forced ending of the friendship after learning that Heinz had joined the German Army and didn't survive the war.

Upon his arrival, the wife of Walter's landlord came to his room an informed him that Nazi authorities had been looking for him. They were rounding up all Jewish men of sound body. Rumor had it, that the men were to be taken to concentration camps to be used as forced labor. The Nazi officer had also reminded her that it was considered a crime to harbor Walter in any way. She thought it would be better if Walter didn't tell her his destination. Minutes later Walter received a call from Tea Jaegerman. She had been frantic about the violence and pleaded for Walter to come stay at their apartment. Walter hesitated, but when her father insisted, he packed his belongings into a single suitcase and bicycled to the Jaegermans. The series of attacks on November 9th and 10th throughout Germany were only concerned with German and Austrian Jews. Because the Jaegermans were Romanian Jews and Romania at the time was a German ally, their apartment became a safehouse for Walter to spend his last few days in Hamburg.

Kristallnacht in Frankfurt

At the very moment Walter was watching the destruction of the Hamburg synagogue, his mother and father were living a different kind of nightmare in their Frankfurt townhouse. Walter's father, Julius was a prosperous businessman in Frankfurt. At the conclusion of World War I, Julius bought Wittwe Hassan, a retail shop from a Turkish widow who wanted to leave Germany. The shop, which sold coffee, chocolate and wine was quite successful. Ten years later Julius owned a chain of thirty-six Wittwe Hassan stores in and around Frankfurt. By 1933 Julius Sommer had become an affluent and well-respected member of the Frankfurt business community. For a farm boy with an eighth-grade education and no money to start with, he had done well for himself. Julius was a German patriot and was optimistic about the future. He was an active member in civic organizations and in the 1933 Julius Sommer was asked to drive Nazi officials in the Mayday Parade in his brand-new Buick convertible. A year later it was illegal for him to fly the German flag on his front porch. He had held out hope that the bad times would pass, but eventuality Julius, the staunch nationalist, realized there was no longer a future for his family under the Nazis.

By November 9, 1938, Julius had divested himself of all but twelve of his Wittwe Hassan stores. He sold the shops to some of the store managers and other entrepreneurs for pennies on the dollar. The final twelve stores were all adorned with a white Star of David painted on the front window which served as a bullseye for the mobs to focus their wrath on the evening of Kristallnacht.

By ten o'clock that evening, Julius Sommer's remaining twelve stores had been destroyed. As he sat quietly with wife Helen, contemplating the events of that day, they heard a knock on the door. It was a local policeman that they had known for several years. The constable had a look of regret on his face. He told them that he had a warrant to arrest Julius at midnight. Despite the years of friendship there was nothing he could do. He warned

Julius to pack a suitcase, wear his warmest clothes and to eat a herty meal. There was no telling how long it would be before he would eat again.

Being the good hostess, Helen Sommer insisted that the policeman stay to share a cup of coffee and eat a piece of apple kuchen until it was time to go. The policeman reluctantly accepted the invitation and at the conclusion of eating the kuchen, escorted Julius to the local police station. From all around Frankfurt able-bodied Jewish men were gathered and forced to stand at attention in the cold night air with nothing to eat or drink.. Shortly before dawn Julius Sommer was loaded onto a cattle car and started on a train ride of his own. The destination was the concentration camp at Buchenwald.

The morning after the Kristallnacht Riots

November 10, 1938

WALTER SOMMERS SPENT THE NIGHT of November 9th on the Jaegerman's couch but was unable to get more than a few minutes of sleep. The reality of what he had witnessed was beginning to hit home. Yesterday had begun as just another workday. Today Walter had awakened to a different world. The lines had been drawn and he was standing on what appeared to be the losing side.

Walter didn't know if the riots had only taken place in Hamburg or had been staged against Jewish communities in other cities as well. He tried to call home to Frankfurt, but the phone lines were not working. Walter, normally filled with teenage bravado, was unsure of which path to take. The safest thing he could do was stay in the Jaegerman's apartment until things calmed down. Another option was to go to work as usual and either wait to see if Kristallnacht was a random act or make arrangements to leave on the next freighter bound for Latin America. Eventually Walter decided it would be safer to go to the offices of Maass & Reige and learn what he could and therefore make an informed decision about his future.

Upon arrival, Walter was immediately sent to a freighter at the port that was scheduled to depart for Costa Rica. He was assigned to compile the ship's inventory with instructions, not to leave the ship until night time. If things got bad, Walter would have the option to hide in the ship until it was in international waters. The Captain had been informed that Walter had secured employment in the Maass and Reige's foreign office and didn't need an exit visa.

Remarkably, at days end, Hamburg seemed to be back to normal. Walter wasn't ready to leave Germany or say goodbye to Tea Jaegerman. He jumped on his bicycle and pedaled past the ruins of the downtown shopping district. Walter fought back tears as he reached the smoldering timbers of the once beautiful Synagogue. It confirmed what he had been thinking about all day. It was too dangerous to remain in Hamburg.

Walter understood his only options were to leave on the next boat for the Western Hemisphere or return to his family in Frankfurt. Without any word from home, he didn't know if circumstances were any better in Frankfurt than Hamburg. He realized that Tea Jaegerman and her family wouldn't be happy with either one of those choices. That night Walter received a phone call from Frankfurt that made his decision for him.

Walter could tell by the tone of his mother's voice that something was wrong. "The Nazi's have taken your father to Buchenwald. You must come home as soon as possible." Her voice was emotional and full of desperation. He realized his mother and sister Lore were helpless to deal with the situation. Walter was dutybound. He needed to return to Frankfurt seek his father's release and obtain exit visas for his family.

On the next morning, Walter packed his suitcase and said a tearful goodbye to Tea Jaegerman and pedaled his bicycle to the train station.

Note Walter was able to move around Hamburg freely at the time of Kristallnacht because the Jewish population had not yet been required to wear the yellow patch in shape of the Star of David with the word, JUDE, prominently displayed. Walter admitted that if he had been forced to wear the patch at that time, he would have no other choice but to flee to Costa Rica or Argentina and leave his family behind.

How Implementing the Jewish Badge Helped the Nazis

The obvious benefit of the badge to the Nazis was the visual labeling of the Jews. No longer would the rabble only be able to attack and persecute those Jews with stereotypical Jewish features or forms of dress, now all Jews and part-Jews were open to the various Nazi actions.

The badge made a distinction. One day there were just people on the street, and the next day, there were Jews and non-Jews.

Reason for Kristallnacht

The assassination of a German diplomat by a 17-year-old German-born Polish Jew provided the pretext for the Nazi attacks on November 9,1938. Kristallnacht was the turning point for Jews in Germany, giving Hitler the excuse he had been waiting for to openly wage a campaign of terror against the Jews.

Aftermath of Kristallnacht The Night of Broken Glass

On the train to Frankfurt

November 15, 1938

THE SOUND OF STEAM BEING released from the locomotive jostled Walter from a restless sleep as the train began to slow down. His first thought was that his identity had been discovered, but when the conductor announced "Hauptbahnhof Hanover," he breathed a sigh of relief. Hanover was a regular stop on the Frankfurt train. Walter looked at his watch and realized he had five or six hours yet to go. There would be a short layover while the engine took on coal and water, but Walter had already decided to stay in his seat while the other men left the compartment to stretch their legs and use the facilities. Even though he was surrounded by Nazi's, he felt somewhat safe in the car. Not having been bothered during the first two hours of the trip, he reasoned as long as he kept quiet he would arrive in Frankfurt without incident.

Walter had close calls with the Nazis before while working at Maas & Reige. One day when he was instructed to make a bank deposit. It took him longer to get there than he had anticipated, so he picked up a tomato from a fruit stand to eat it whenever he got the chance. Since the bank line was extremely long, he decided to eat the tomato while waiting behind a menacing-looking SS officer. Without thinking, he took a huge bite out of the tomato and then heard a collective gasp from everyone standing behind him. Horrified, Walter saw that the juicy tomato had spattered all over the back of the SS officer's uniform. "I thought I was good as dead," Walter admitted. "An SS officer was above the law and if he found out I was a Jew— he could send me to a concentration camp. I didn't know whether to stay in line or run. I just stood there. Fortunately, everybody in the bank was as frightened as I was. The SS Officer did his business and walked out. Five minutes later, I did the same and ran back to the office. I have often wondered what that officer thought when he found his uniform had been stained with tomato juicw. I was just glad I wasn't there to find out."

Walter feigned sleep when the five Nazi's returned to the compartment just as the train was leaving the station. They smelled of Schnapps and cigarette smoke and were laughing as they settled back into their seats. They acted as if they didn't have a care in the world. Walter found it odd that German Christians had been able go about their life as usual under Adolf Hitler while Walter's family, who had also been loyal Germans, were about to lose everything for being Jewish.

Walter's thoughts wandered back to a time when he had never heard the term anti-Semitic; a time before the Nazis when his family prospered in their beloved Germany. His future then seemed bright and limitless. Seven years later, that Germany had become a fading memory.

Before Hitler

Walter was born on December 29, 1920, as the first child of Julius and Helen Sommer. Julius was from the small town of Heinebach which was about an hour north of Frankfurt. After eight years of education in a one room schoolhouse, Julius's father secured him an apprenticeship at a department

Salomon, Ernest, & Julius Sommer

store in Frankfurt. At the age of fourteen, Julius moved from the serene Hessian countryside to the fast-paced life at one of Germany's largest cities. Julius did well for himself, but the outbreak of World War I saw him drafted into the Wehrmacht. Due to his department store experience, he was assigned as a quartermaster. His older brothers, Ernest, and Salomon. were also drafted into the army and both became decorated infantry men. Julius, though, was given a medical discharge after a botched appendicitis surgery.

Soon after his medical discharge he married his paternal first cousin Helen, one of three daughters of a school teacher from the village of Kassel. Like Julius, Helen was a proud nationalist who saw herself as German first and Jewish second. As the German Army advanced to within a few miles of Paris, Helen started making her victory quilt to commemorate the end of the war. However, the United States entry into the war forced Germany to surrender. The armistice, known as the Treaty of Versailles, imposed harsh sanctions and reparations on Germany which planted the seeds of resentment that the Nazi Party exploited to come to power.

However, in the postwar years Julius used his savings to purchase an apartment building along with a small retail shop from a widow who wanted to return to Turkey. The store was aptly named Wittwe Hassan, or when translated: Widow Hassan. The store sold fine coffee, Swiss and German chocolates, and local German wines.

Julius bought Turkish coffee beans and hand sorted through them, discarding any bean that didn't measure up. He then roasted and ground the beans into the finished product. Wine was shipped to the store in fifty-gallon wooden kegs, stored in the backroom and basement, and tapped to fill whatever size bottle the customer provided. Chocolate was imported from Switzerland and prepared by local confectionaries. Every product was carefully weighed, measured, and packaged to each customer's specifications. Julius's formula was extremely successful and over the years he was able to open thirty-six Wittwe Hassan stores in and around Frankfurt.

Julius and Helen lived frugally and saved every mark they earned. However, when Walter was born in 1920, Julius wanted the best for his son and money wasn't a factor when it came to Walter's well-being. One of the first problems the young parents encountered was a shortage of milk. As a result of the Treaty of Versailles severe reparations were imposed against Germany. Most of the dairy cows in Western Germany were confiscated and taken to France. The few remaining cows fell far short of meeting the needs of sixty-two million Germans. For those lucky enough to find a bottle of milk, the price would be too high to purchase. Julius was determined that Walter would not go without milk. To solve the problem he went to the countryside, purchased a Holstein milk cow and under the

Walter and Lore

cover of darkness, moved the cow in the basement of his apartment building. Baby Walter got all the milk he needed. "I don't think the tenants were happy in the beginning," Walter explained. "But when they realized the cow produced enough milk and cream for the entire building, they decided that the cow was a good thing." Shortly afterward, Julius added chickens to the basement menagerie, and the building enjoyed a daily supply of eggs with their milk.

Walter's sister, Lore, was born in 1924. Julius moved the family to a row house in an affluent section of Frankfurt. Walter described the area as being "upper middle class." The house was more appropriate for a man of Julius standing in the community, whether Jewish or Gentile. This house would be Walter's home until he left Frankfurt.

The Haircut

Julius was head of the household in the traditional German manner, Helen was in charge of rearing the children. "She was a strict disciplinarian, but she always had my best interest in mind." Walter smiled and admitted, "I guess I was what you would call a Mama's boy."

Walter Before Haircut   *After Haircut*

Despite being a Mama's boy, Walter was strong-willed and adamant about what he wanted. At the age of four, Helen learned just how far Walter was willing to go to get his way. Helen saw Walter as her baby, but Walter saw himself as a boy and wanted to look the part. Unfortunately, Helen insisted on keeping Walter's hair long and fashioned in a way that was more appropriate for a toddler. "It made me look like a girl and I wanted a boy's haircut," Walter declared. Julius was on Walter's side, but Helen had the deciding vote. Her answer was an emphatic, "No."

After holding his breath and not getting the answer he wanted by turning blue, Walter waited until his mother was busy with his baby sister and slipped out the front door without being noticed. He ran around the corner of a busy Frankfurt intersection and found the barbershop which his father frequented biweekly. Walter walked into the store and delivered his ultimatum. "I want a big boy's haircut."

The barber was taken aback by the strong-willed boy, but soon recognized Walter as Julius's son. After assuring the barber that he had his parent's permission, and that his father would pay for the haircut later, the barber cut Walter's hair above his ears in the manner worn by most preteen German boys of that time.

Walter and Julius Hiking in the Tanus Mountain

Meanwhile, Helen began to panic when she realized Walter wasn't in the house. She looked on the sidewalk and didn't see him anywhere. She looked inside the house one last time and then realized what Walter had done. She ran immediately to the barber shop and burst into tears as Walter's last remaining curl fell to the floor. Walter knew he was in big trouble, but he had the boy's haircut he so desperately wanted. "I had never seen my mother that angry before, and began to question my decision, but what could I do?" Walter reasoned. "I remember being sent to my room for what seemed a lifetime, but when my father arrived at home and learned what had happened, he was on my side. I was four years old and no longer a baby. I needed to look like a boy."

The Sommer's family belonged to the Haupt Synagogue in Frankfurt. Walter described it as the first semi-reformed synagogue in the city. "Men wore hats in temple but not yarmulkes," Walter explained. "I didn't know what a yarmulke was until we arrived in New York City. The services were delivered in German with only a little bit of Hebrew. The Bar Mitzvahs were similar to what you would see in America today." Walter described his family as high holiday Jews. "We celebrated the Big Four major Jewish Holidays, Rosh Hashana, Yom-Kippur, Chanukah and Passover." The Sommer Family also celebrated Christmas. "I had the best of both worlds," Walter explained. "My sister and I received presents during Chanukah and Christmas too."

With the exception of a model train, Walter remembered most of his toys being homemade. "It wasn't like my father couldn't afford it. It was just the way things were done back them." One of Walter's most memorable gifts was a .410 shotgun he received from his maternal Grandfather, Isaac, for his fifth birthday. "We dressed up in hunting clothes and hunted for pheasant in the Frankfurt City Park." Walter was proud of his Grandfather who was a war hero in the Franco-Prussian wsar in 1870.

Walter's Education

After reaching a moderate level of success, Julius who had only been able to attend school until the eighth grade in a one room schoolhouse, decided that Walter was going to get the best education available in Frankfurt. After four years in a Jewish grade school, Julius secured Walter a spot in the prestigious private Muster-Schule. Muster-Schule which means 'sample school' was the most progressive high school in the city with every teacher required to have a doctorate degree. Instead of teaching the traditional classic languages of Greek and Latin, Muster Schule taught their students French at age ten, English at eleven, Spanish at twelve and finally Latin at age fourteen. "It was the only school in town that taught about the world outside of Germany," Walter explained and credited his knowledge of foreign languages as the reason he looked at the world from a different perspective than his father.

Dr. Hoffman's Class at Muster Schule. Walter is next to top row, third from the right

Julius had learned about the world in a country one-room schoolhouse and in the battlefields of France. He spoke only German and had always lived in or around Frankfurt. When Walter learned English, he learned about America on the other side of the Atlantic Ocean. He learned about the founding fathers named Washington, Jefferson and Franklin. He also learned about America through the movies that came to local theatres. To Walter America seemed like a

Back on the train to Frankfurt

November 15, 1938

WALTER RECOGNIZED THE RAILROAD STATION as the train pulled into the City of Kassel. It was his mother's hometown. He had nothing but fond memories of holidays with his family in Kassel but found no pleasure in tonight's visit. He was less than two hours away from life in post-Kristall-nacht Frankfurt. Walter had been worried about his father's well-being, but up until now nothing seemed real from afar in Hamburg. As the train neared Frankfurt he was beginning to realize the danger he and his family were facing. His father had been sent to Buchenwald and it was up to Walter to get him out.

Three of the Nazi's stepped out of the compartment during the lay-over in Kassel, while the other two slept. Walter waited for a few minutes before using the restroom. As he searched for the toilet, he noticed that a third of the passengers had disembarked. He hoped the three Soldiers who had left his compartment were no longer on the train, but they were back in their seats upon Walter's return. He willed himself to remain calm and keep his mouth shut until he reached Frankfurt. Walter realized how hungry he was as he watched one of the soldiers eat a liverwurst sandwich. Why did he have to suffer, just for being Jewish? It wasn't fair that the Nazi could eat liverwurst while he went hungry. He began to feel sorry for himself, then he remembered where his father was. There wasn't a Jew in Nazi Germany, who hadn't heard of a concentration camp. However, very few had any information about the conditions inside. Walter fell into this category. He didn't know what his father was enduring but was convinced it wasn't good. His hunger paled in comparison to what his father was going through.

Julius on the way to Buchenwald

After being forced to stand at attention without food and water in a large public hall, Julius Sommer was forced to march to the train yard with other Jewish prisoners rounded up on Kristallnacht. Even though Julius was 50 years old at the time, he was in better shape than many of the other prisoners, thanks to the warning of his arresting officer. The hearty meal Helen had prepared had given him sufficient strength to stay on his feet while others much younger than him had collapsed while waiting for the train. Those who fell to the ground were mercilessly kicked and beaten until other prisoners helped them back to their feet. It was dark and the temperature was below freezing on the night of November 10, when the train finally arrived, Julius had been on his feet for twenty-four hours.

Dozens of SS troopers descended from the train, armed with machine guns and German Shepherd attack dogs. Railroad workers opened the doors and lowered livestock ramps to the ground, as soldiers began to herd the prisoners into the open-air cattle cars. Prisoners who weren't moving fast enough were struck with the butt of a rifle or bitten by one of the attack dogs. In a matter of mere seconds, the cattle cars were full, and the doors were closed and chained shut.

Train to Buchenwald

There was barely enough room to sit, but Julius was grateful to get off of his feet. He was also grateful for the warning from the local constable. Not only was he wearing his warmest winter coat, but also a wool scarf fur-lined gloves and fur hat. Many of the other prisoners had been taken from their homes without a coat at all.

Julius had always been a staunch German nationalist, so the humiliation of the past two days must have seemed beyond surreal. Despite Walter's constant warnings and the onslaught of anti-Semitic laws, he couldn't fathom that his beloved Germany was capable of such atrocities. Unfortunately, the Holocaust had just begun.

The prisoners weren't given any information as to their destination and the guards made it clear that there where consequences for speaking without being spoken to. After waiting in silence for several more hours the train finally started the two-hundred-mile trek eastward to Buchenwald. Julius Sommer, a man who had enjoyed a comfortable lifestyle and was held in high regard by his community, now found himself with the same rights and privileges of a dairy cow. In actuality, the dairy cow was held in higher esteem in the eyes of the Nazis.

The train came to a stop in the pre-dawn darkness near the town of Weimar in the state of Thuringia. None of the prisoners knew where they were. Suddenly, the doors flew open, and Julius was ordered out of the car where he was struck with rifle butts and beaten with buggy whips. Attack dogs were unleashed on the prisoners while soldiers instructed them to line up next to the train. After a few minutes of terror, the prisoners found themselves standing at attention waiting as a series of roll calls were taken. Julius and the other prisoners were still at attention several hours later. As Julius would learn, standing at attention in both good and bad weather was one of the Nazi's preferred methods of torture in Buchenwald.

As the sun reached what appeared to be noon, Julius was lined up with the other prisoners and marched on a dirt road through a dense forest of beech trees. After a half hour he realized he was at the Buchenwald Concentration Camp. Walking through the camp entrance he was puzzled by the sign at the gate, -JADEM DAS SEINE, when translated means "to each their own." The phrase itself doesn't seem so ominous, but the Nazis viewed the meaning as Aryans with Aryans and Jews with Jews. Taken one step further it meant, Aryans as the Master Race could do what they wanted with the Jews. And that is exactly how things went at Buchenwald.

After being taken to a processing center, Julius was stripped of everything in his possession, including his clothes and coat. In their stead he was given a blue and grey threadbare jacket, trousers, cap, and wooden clogs. Once in uniform, he was forced to stand in formation while waiting assignment to a barrack. It was over twenty-four hours since any of the Frankfurt prisoners had been given any food or water. Whenever a prisoner grew weak and collapsed they were beaten until they stepped back into formation. Finally, at two in the morning each prisoner was given a small tin of sardines but no water. Shortly afterward Julius and the others were assigned to a barrack and were allowed to sleep, three men per bunk. Julius and the other prisoners were standing back in formation attention shortly after dawn.

Mornings at Buchenwald

The day usually began between 4am and 4.30am when prisoners were awakened in their barracks. They had between 30-45 minutes to dress, use the toilet, make their beds, clean the barracks, and eat breakfast. Toilet and washing facilities, where there was usually only dirty water, and no soap or toilet paper were shared by up to 2000 prisoners. Anyone who completed these tasks too slowly faced punishment.

Roll Call at Buchenwald

Prisoners then lined up for the morning roll call, a registration of all prisoners in the camp, including those who had died in the night or those that were ill. The prisoners would be counted twice, and any discrepancies resulted in a recount. The morning roll call could take hours. Throughout this time, prisoners had to endure extreme German winter weather. Any prisoners that collapsed or were found to be missing faced beatings, torture, or execution.

For lunch Julius was given a small bowl of watery vegetable soup. After spending the afternoon on a work crew Julius returned to the barracks where he received a larger bowl of soup along with a slice of bread. Within days Julius began to lose weight from the low-calorie count and developed a cough from standing in the cold for hours at a time without a coat or hat. He was coming down with pneumonia. Julius Sommer was a strong man, but realized that he wouldn't last long if his family was unable to secure his release.

Buchenwald Concentration Camp

The Buchenwald Concentration Camp was constructed in July of 1937 near the City of Weimar in central Germany. Eventually it became one of the largest concentration camps in Germany. The first internees were actual or suspected Communists. This was followed by political prisoners, and then the physically disabled and mentally ill individuals whom the Nazis considered to be a drain on society. However, in 1938, in the aftermath of Kristallnacht, German SS and police sent almost 10,000 Jews to Buchenwald where the camp authorities subjected them to extraordinarily cruel treatment upon arrival. 255 of them died as a result of their initial mistreatment at the camp. Buchenwald's purpose was to provide slave labor for local ammunition and armament factories in the area. Since the supply of prisoners seemed endless, It was camp policy to provide the prisoners enough food to keep them working for a period of two months, during which many if not most starved to death. By the time Buchenwald was liberated by the 6th Armored Division of the United States Army, 56,545 of the 285,000 prisoners who had entered through the gates of Buchenwald had been murdered by the Waffen SS.

Walter arrives in Frankfurt

It was well past midnight as the Hamburg train pulled into the Frankfurt Hauptbahnhof. Walter waited until the Stormtroopers left the compartment before making his way back to the baggage car. He brought his claim check and stood in line while the porters unloaded the trunks and suitcases. When Walter's bicycle and suitcase arrived at the door, he once again had trouble lifting it to the ground. One of the Stormtroopers who had been riding in Walter's compartment recognized his predicament and help Walter unload his bike from the train. "He couldn't have been any nicer," Walter remembered. "He helped me load my suitcase onto the bicycle and wished me luck. The thought that I might be a Jew never entered his mind."

Frankfurt was still bustling even though it was the middle of the night. It was two years since he had been home. Everything looked familiar, but Frankfurt was different. Buildings were covered with Nazi banners and propaganda. As he reached the central business district, he was shocked by the devastation of what had once been filled with Jewish owned stores. Among the burned and looted buildings was one of his father's Wittwe

Hassan stores. The windows were all broken, and the fixtures and inventory had been looted. It was one thing to see the damage done in Hamburg on Kristallnacht, but the damage in Frankfurt seemed more personal in nature. His father had worked a lifetime building a chain of retail stores and now they were all in ruin. This was his city. These were his people. How could they do this?

A tear formed on his cheek as he passed by his school. His father had been proud of the education Walter had received in the esteemed private institution. The Muster Schule had provided Walter with the skills he needed to get ahead in Germany only to have Germany take that world away from him.

As Walter walked past the athletic field he remembered how proud he was to be a member of the field hockey team. He spent countless days running on the track and throwing the javelin after school. He was just one of the boys at Muster-Schule before he was singled out. One day after school in 1935, the coach told him that the Jews were no longer allowed to participate with the team. It was a bitter pill for him to swallow.

Walter at Muster Schule

"The only thing that lessened the pain was that I was able to join an all-Jewish field hockey team," Walter explained. "We played my old club and beat them soundly. They took the loss like good sports. Surprisingly, there wasn't any hatred at that time."

The Hitler Youth Organization took the place of the Boy Scouts in Germany. When a Nazi Party Official came to school to recruit boys for the Hitler Youth, Walter wanted to join. "He made it sound so exciting," Walter explained. "I tried to sign up. There was hiking and swimming while camping in the mountains. It all sounded like a wonderful adventure. But when the recruiter learned I was a Jew, he told me I wasn't wanted."

Since Jewish boys weren't allowed in the Hitler Youth Organization, The Little Black Flag Organization became the Jewish Boy Scouts. "We wore black pants, and our camp was right next to the Nazi camp," Walter remembered. "Amazingly, all the boys got along fine in the beginning. But as the years passed and the Hitler Youth became indoctrinated into the Nazi Party, things changed, and we were looked down upon as being less than human."

Prohibiting Jews from joining youth organizations and school sports clubs was one of the first acts of Nazi oppression after they gained control of the country. As late as May 1, 1933, Julius Sommers was still participating in the May Day Parade by driving Nazi Officials in his new Buick convertible. The expulsion from his sports club was the first deep cut in Walter's life. In 1936 Walter was forced to leave his beloved Muster-Schule entirely. The only option left was for him to attend a nearby Jewish School.

Walter was heartbroken to leave his classmates at Muster-Schule but quickly learned that the student body at the Jewish High School included girls. At age 16, the experience of interacting with girls took some of the sting out of leaving his school. Before long Walter struck up a fond friendship with a classmate named Eva, the daughter of a prominent lawyer, who apparently felt the same way. However, under the strict eye of the headmaster, there wasn't much chance for a romance to blossom. Despite laws that restricted Jewish movement, both Walter and Eva told their parents that their class was taking a field trip when in fact school was closed for the day. Their parents didn't suspect a thing when the couple played hooky and went hiking in the Taunus Mountains. Decades later in a conversation with his son Ron, Walter admitted that they got away with the adventure without getting caught. When Ron asked if all they did was hike that day, Walter turned red and admitted that he stole a kiss. "We were in love." Many years later Walter met Eva who had escaped to America and settled in Chicago. "She was a little old lady and apparently I was more impressed with the love affair than she was."

Returning to Frankfurt after two years in Hamburg was a double-edged sword for Walter as far as memories were concerned. Pleasant memories of his maternal grandfather taking him pheasant hunting in the park came to mind. Walter had received a shotgun for his 5th birthday and to celebrate his grandfather bundled him up and took him off into the woods in chase of birds. It was a wonderful memory. However as he passed a park bench he was reminded how bad things had become under the Nazi regime. A sign next to the bench read. NO DOGS or JEWS ALLOWED ON BENCH!

He remembered shared adventures through the park at twelve years of age with his first girlfriend, Renata Addleman. After riding bikes they would go to Walter's house for cookies and milk. Walter liked Renata, despite the fact his mother complained she had thick thighs. "She was a nice girl from a nice family," Walter explained. "Her father was a well-respected judge in Frankfurt. Unfortunately, the Nazis created a law that said Jews could not hold a government office. He lost his job and became destitute. The last I heard; their family ended up in a camp."

Even the act of returning home was a reminder of what he had lost. Two years earlier when Walter left to start his apprenticeship in Hamburg, he left from the family's upscale house at 5 Loenstrasse in one of Frankfurt's prestigious neighborhoods. Shortly after his departure, the Nazi's made it illegal for Jews to own a single-family home. Julius was forced to sell his home for a fraction of its value and move back into the three-unit apartment building at 32 Finkelhof Strasse he had purchased at the end of World War I.

Julius was a proud patriot and always flew a German flag outside of the front door. He was proud that he and his two brothers served in German Army during World War I and was in favor of a strong Germany. He joined the veterans clubs and participated in every May Day parade by driving Nazi officials in his Buick convertible.

Julius Sommer in his first car

That ended as the Nazi's enacted a series of laws that systematically stripped the Jewish population of their rights. Wealth or status had no bearing when it came to these laws. Even Ludwig Landmann, the Jewish Mayor of Frankfurt was stripped of his office and forced to flee to The Netherlands.

*** After Germany invaded The Netherlands, Landmann was forced to hide in the same area as Anne Frank, where he died of starvation in 1945. ***

After building successful business and serving in the German Army, Julius had lost his home, 36 retail stores, and his German citizenship. Now he was residing in a concentration camp. Walter had witnessed what the SA mobs did to the Jews in Hamburg. As far as he knew; his father could be dead. Despite the odds, he was determined to save his father.

When Walter arrived home in the middle of the night, his mother, Helen was waiting with open arms. "She was obviously upset about my father's arrest, but she was single-mindedly focused on doing everything possible to secure his release," Walter recalled. "She cooked me a nice meal and sent me to bed with the knowledge I was to go to work first thing in the morning. It was my job to find a way out of Germany for my family."

While Helen Sommer wanted Walter to concentrate on getting visas for the family, Walter was keenly aware of one family member who might not be going. His father's sister, Miriam was disabled and unable to walk without the aid of crutches. Miriam, called Mimi by Walter and his sister Lore, had lived with the family before Walter's birth. Mimi suffered from severe arthritis as a young woman and under the care of a small village doctor was placed in a pair of casts where both knees were set in a bent position. When the casts were removed Mimi was unable to straighten her legs. The doctors in Frankfurt tried to repair her legs but couldn't. The damage was irreversible.

Miriam Sommer did not let her handicap slow her down. She kept the books for Wittwe Hassan without the aid of an adding machine. "She used to add several triple-digit-numbers in her head," Walter bragged. She was one of the smartest women I have ever known. As his father's older sister, Miriam often overruled Walter's disciplinarian mother. After a trip to Greece, Miriam brought a large ornate pocket knife to Walter as a gift. His mother was furious, but Aunt Mimi insisted that he keep the knife since it came all the way from Greece. "There was quite a bit of friction between my mother and my aunt," Walter explained. "For the most part Mimi was always on my side." Walter had to do everything in his power to get Mimi the visa.

Until 1936 Julius Sommers believed that Germany would eventually come to its senses and vote Hitler and the Nazis out of power. But when the Nuremberg Laws were enacted, he had to admit Walter was right. The family needed to leave Germany. Walter had always lobbied for the family to immigrate to the United States, but soon found out it was difficult to do so.

Even the Rabbi who officiated at Walter's Bar Mitzvah seemed to be working against Walter's efforts to come to America. "I stood up in front of the congregation and read from the Torah like I was supposed to do," Walter remembered. "But instead of getting up and talking about me, the

Rabbi starting preaching about how we as Jews couldn't allow Hitler to run us out of Germany. 'We are Germans, and we must stay in Germany!' he shouted. On our way home my father pounded his fist on the steering wheel and said 'That's it! We are staying! The Rabbi is never wrong!" To Walter, America seemed a million miles away.

Walter's Bar Mitzvah portrait

Documents Required to Obtain a Visa

German Jews attempting to immigrate to the United States in the late 1930s faced overwhelming bureaucratic hurdles. It was difficult to procure the necessary papers to leave Germany. The process could take years. As the Nazi regime's attacks intensified in the late 1930s, hundreds of thousands of Jews in Germany tried to immigrate to the United States. To enter the United States, each person needed an immigration visa stamped into his or her passport.

Nations required extensive documentation that was often virtually impossible to obtain. The following is a list of the documents required by the United States to obtain a visa.

Five copies of the visa application

Two copies of the applicant's birth certificate

Quota number (establishing the applicant's place on the waiting list)

Two sponsors:

Close relatives of the prospective immigrant were preferred.

The sponsors were required to be US citizens or to have permanent resident status, and they were required to have completed and notarized six copies of an Affidavit of Support and Sponsorship

Supporting documents:

Certified copy of most recent federal tax return

Affidavit from a bank regarding applicant's accounts

Affidavit from any other responsible person regarding other assets (affidavit from sponsor's employer or statement of commercial rating)

Certificate of Good Conduct from German Police authorities, including two copies of each:

Police dossier

Prison record

Military record

Other government records about individual

Affidavits of Good Conduct from several responsible disinterested persons

Physical examination at US consulate

Proof of permission to leave Germany.

Proof that prospective immigrant had booked passage to the Western hemisphere.

As the refugee crisis began in 1938, growing competition for a finite number of visas, affidavits, and travel options made immigration even more difficult. In June 1938, 139,163 people were on the waiting list for the German quota. One year later, in June 1939, the waiting list had jumped to 309,782.

> It was becoming more and more evident that Jews, should leave if anybody at all would have them, and not very many countries would have them.
>
> —Kurt Klein

During 1938–1939, in a program known as the Kindertransport, the United Kingdom admitted 10,000 unaccompanied Jewish children on an emergency basis. 1939 also marked the first time the United States filled its combined German-Austrian quota. However, this limit did not come close to meeting the demand; by June 1939, 309,000 German, Austrian, and Czech Jews had applied for the 27,000 places available under the quota.

The events of 1938 caused a dramatic increase in Jewish immigration. The German annexation of Austria in March, increasing personal assaults on Jews during the spring and summer, the nationwide Kristallnacht pogrom in November, and subsequent seizure of Jewish-owned property all caused a flood of visa applications. Although finding a destination proved difficult, about 36,000 Jews left Germany and Austria in 1938 and 77,000 in 1939.

By September 1939, approximately 282,000 Jews had left Germany and 117,000 from annexed Austria. Of these, some 95,000 emigrated to the United States, 60,000 to Palestine, 40,000 to Great Britain, and about 75,000 to Central and South America, with the largest numbers entering Argentina, Brazil, Chile, and Bolivia. More than 18,000 German Jews were also able to find refuge in Shanghai, in Japanese-occupied China.

Walter Struggles to Find Visas

The one major problem Walter had to overcome was that his family's lack of relatives living in the United States. Starting in 1935 Walter urged his father to search for relatives in America who would sponsor the family to immigrate. Julius eventually agreed and wrote letters to every known relative, but none were able or willing to sponsor his family. Coming up empty, Julius explained that nothing could be done. The family would simply have to endure life in Germany under the Nazis.

A distant cousin of Walters went to America for a visit in 1936 and a family reunion was scheduled for the day of his return. With conditions worsening for the Jews, everybody wanted to know whether the United States was the new land of milk and honey. To Walter's dismay the report couldn't have been more negative. "My cousin went to Cleveland and absolutely hated everything about the trip. He had gone in June in the midst of a heat wave and reported America was too hot and humid and there was massive unemployment and a lack of jobs. According to my cousin, there was no way to make money to live on. After my father heard that, he said "That's it. We are staying. At that point I was ready to give up on persuading my parents to immigrate to the United States."

Unhappy with the answer, Walter asked his father to try writing cousins of our cousins. Julius sighed, but realized Walter would pester him until he followed through. So, Julius did follow through and much to his surprise, received an answer from a cousin named, Stern, who had a cousin in Hoboken, New Jersey who had been willing to sponsor him. Julius wrote this cousin of his cousin, who was also named Stern and was surprised when he received a positive response. He said he would fill out all of the necessary paperwork to bring them to America, but in no way could he help the Sommer family financially. "He wasn't being cruel and stingy," Walter explained. "America was still in the midst of the depression. It was all he could afford to offer. He was struggling to make ends meet for his on family. He told us to come to his house as soon as we arrived at the dock, and he would put us up for the night and provide a nice meal. After that, we would be on our own. We were extremely grateful for what he offered."

After completing the paper work, nothing happened for months. They didn't realize it at the time, but the waiting list for German immigrants was over 100,000. "While working in Hamburg, I had almost given up hope." Now that Julius was in Buchenwald, an exit visa was desperately needed more than ever.

When Walter returned to Frankfurt after Kristallnacht, he focused on securing his Father's release from Buchenwald. On his first morning back Helen cooked him breakfast and told him to go to the British Consulate and see if he could secure exit visas to England.

Before going to the British Consulate, Walter visited with his faithful ally Aunt Miriam. Promising that he would do everything possible to secure a visa for her, though she was resigned to the fact that she would be staying in Germany. She said that no country wanted an old, crippled woman like her. The thought of leaving his beloved aunt behind rendered Walter heartbroken, She assured him that she would be fine and that it was his job to get his father out of the concentration camp and then out of the country.

Walter surveyed the damage done on Kristallnacht to Frankfurt's business district. Everything seemed surreal. The department stores that Walter had frequented during his youth had been burned, looted, and left as rubble. The beautiful synagogues with priceless scrolls and artifacts had been destroyed. Worst of all was the damage that was done to his father's Wittwe Hassan shops throughout the city. "Up until then everyone in our neighborhood was German. Nobody asked if we were Jewish," Walter lamented. "Before the Nazis came to power, we lived together and got along with one another. At that point there wasn't any doubt that the Jewish population had been designated for persecution."

When Walter reached the British Consulate he became distraught. Hundreds of people were standing in line, all desperate for an exit visa. For years ominous storm clouds had been forming in Frankfurt. Unfortunately, many others like Julius Sommer were convinced that they could weather the storm and hadn't taken heed of the warning signs. "The Nazis will come and go. This is only a temporary condition! We've had several governments since the Great War. Mark my words. Hitler will be gone before you know it!"

The Kristallnacht Pogrom had changed everything. The period in time which would later be known as the Holocaust had begun. For years Walter had warned his family to leave and now hoped that it wasn't too late.

Walter hadn't left for South America when he had the chance, choosing to return from Hamburg to save his family. But after looking at all the people ahead of him in line, he prayed he hadn't allowed himself to be caught in a trap that that was designed to eliminate every Jew in Germany.

After two hours the line at the British Consulate hadn't moved at all. Just when Walter was ready to give up, a British Official appeared and announced that all people who could speak English were told to form a separate line. Out of the hundreds of people in line, only a few dozen spoke English. Walter stepped over to the English-speaking line and within minutes he was ushered into the Consulate of Great Britain. By sundown, Walter had procured exit visas to England for himself, his mother and father along with his sister, Lore. England, however, would not take anyone who needed crutches to walk. There wouldn't be a visa for Aunt Mimi. Now the task at hand was to find a way to get his father, out of Buchenwald.

Julius Sommer was a popular man in Frankfurt. Just prior to Easter in 1934 the Nazi's mandated that every Jewish Store was to be identified with a Star of David on the window. The sign stated: "This is a Jewish store and Germans should not shop here." To make things worse, the Nazis stationed an SA brown-shirted trooper outside the front door to intimidate both German and Jewish customers. Julius feared that would be the end of his business, but it had the opposite effect. German people didn't like to be told what to do. The pushed the brown-shirts out of the way and went into the store. With over 30 stores in Frankfurt Wittwe Hassan was a fixture in many neighborhoods. People wanted to buy coffee, chocolate, and wine from Julius Sommer. Easter season in 1934 turned out to be one of the best in years. Julius even considered expanding, but new anti-Semitic laws seemed to be written every week. Each law was more restrictive. Any idea of expansion was forgotten. All the Jewish Community could do was to try to survive and hope it would pass.

Some Germans who defied the Nazis to buy supplies for their Easter celebration in 1934 still had fond feelings for Julius Sommers. Even though many had joined the Nazi Party out of necessity, there were people willing to help Julius. Walter and his mother contacted some of these Nazi friends and recruited them to help secure Julius's release. They called in favors and sent money to bribe officials hoping to find favor with someone in power. Once everything was put into motion, all they could do was wait.

Two days after Walter secured an exit visa from the British Consulate, he learned that his family had been granted approval to immigrate to the United States of America. He had all but given up hope. He had dreamed of going to America for years and suddenly it seemed to be within his grasp. He prayed that his father would be released before the door to leave Germany was closed permanently. His excitement was dampened when he realized the United States had not lifted their ban on immigrants with infirmities. His Aunt Mimi was going to be left behind.

A week after receiving approval to emigrate to America, the family had not heard a word, positive or negative from Buchenwald. Anxiety was setting in when they heard a knock on the door. It was Julius Sommer. The bribes and efforts of their Nazi friends had been enough to secure his release. "It was the happiest day and also the saddest day of my life at the same time," Walter remembers. "My father was home, but I could barely recognize him. He had pneumonia and had lost so much weight he looked skeletal. It was unbelievable how much he had deteriorated after only a few weeks in a concentration camp." Walter realized that it could have been him if he had been caught up in the SA dragnet on the night of Kristallnacht.

The first order of business was to get Julius healthy enough to pass his physical to go to America. Walter wasn't sure that it would be possible. If rejected, Julius would have to remain in Germany with Mimi. In the meantime, there were things to do before they could leave. Walter rounded up the necessary paperwork and with visas in hand went to Nazi headquarters to secure an exit permit. Once it was deemed that everything was in order, Walter got the word that the Sommer Family had permission to leave.

Walter was amazed how smoothly everything had gone. He knew that wealthy Jewish families were allowed if not encouraged to leave as a way of confiscating their wealth by way of an exit tax. In order for Julius Sommer and his family to leave Germany, he was required to turn over 90 percent of their wealth to the Nazi's. Under the circumstances he was happy to do so.

A few months later, the Nazis didn't even bother to hide their theft of Jewish property under the premise of a tax. They simply took it without reparation.

On the very next day after Walter had procured the exit permits, a SS officer moved into the Sommer household to prevent them from hiding anything of value. The Nazi audited everything in the house down to the last spoon, fork, and candlestick. "The SS officer was a nice man who had a job to do. He was simply following orders. This is a German trait that is difficult for Americans to understand," Walter explained. "Germans followed orders without question. The Nazi's knew this and took advantage of it."

The officer ate lunch with the Sommer family every day and eventually, became a friend of the family.

"Surprisingly, they let us keep the fine China and silverware," Walter said. "They were valuable and could be sold as soon as we reached America.

After the Nazi's took what they wanted the family packed everything they owned into large wooden crates which were sent ahead to the shipping company in Holland. After buying tickets to America, Julius Sommer, the owner of a chain of over 30 retail stores was set to leave Germany with less than 500 dollars in cash. "My father had hidden a few thousand dollars in a Swiss bank, but all we had was our furniture and a little bit of cash."

Even though Julius had always resisted Walter's efforts to immigrate to America, he did recognize the need to set aside some money in the event of an emergency. Each summer he would take the family on a vacation to Switzerland. The Nazis were careful to make sure that large sums of money weren't taken out of the country. But because Julius Sommer was wealthy, he was allowed to take enough money to stay in a nice hotel and eat in fine restaurants. "One we crossed the border, my father got us a room in the cheapest hotel he could find, and we didn't eat at restaurants at all. There were no bathrooms or running water in the rooms. My mother would buy sausages and cheese and we would hike in the mountains and do other things that were free. My father deposited the money into a Swiss bank before returning back to Germany. He intended that this money could be wired to them in America.

After sending the furniture on ahead, the family made plans to go to the American Consulate in Stuttgart to take our physicals and get our visas. "My father was not recovering very well after his weeks at Buchenwald," Walter remembered. "I wasn't sure he would be able to pass the physical. If he didn't pass, he couldn't go to America. My mother would never have gone without him, and I don't know if my sister Lore and I could have gone on alone. There was no other option. We had given everything to the Nazis and what we did own was on a train to Holland. He just had to pass!"

Before the family could leave for Stuttgart, arrangements were made for Mimi to move in with Julius's brother Ernst. After a tearful goodbye, Walter wondered if he would ever see her again. "I felt like I had failed her. I thought maybe we would see each other again when things got back to normal in Germany. I was hopeful, but I was also naive. I never saw my Aunt Mimi again. After the war, I learned that Mimi was murdered at Auschwitz."

After Mimi left there was nothing left to do but get on the train. The 150-mile trip to Stuttgart seemed to last forever. "My father didn't look well," Walter recalls. "He was ashen white and wobbled like an old man. I just prayed he could get through the physical. The train was full of Nazis which added to my parents anxiety. By this time they were all too aware that Nazis didn't need a reason to persecute Jews. My father tried to calm my mother, but he was just as frightened as she was. He held my mother's hand, and I held my sister's as well. We stayed silent and made sure we didn't make eye contact with any of the soldiers. After what seemed like an eternity, we finally arrived at the Stuttgart station."

The American Consulate was a-buzz with activity as the Sommer family approached the last hurdle between them and freedom in America. Their papers were in order with the exception of the physical exams. Julius was putting on a good show, but he still suffered from the physical and psychological damage done at Buchenwald. He tried to walk normally, but in reality he was shuffling like an 80-year-old man. If the doctor preformed a thorough examination, there was no way he would pass. It was unthinkable that they could have come so close and still be denied an exit visa. Having shipped their furniture ahead and no longer having a place to live, they would be destitute and homeless.

Walter was first in line as a pudgy white-haired doctor called him into a cubicle. He looked at Walter, asked him how he felt then sent him on ahead as approved. Lore and Helen went next and were immediately sent to stand with Walter. Finally, it was time for Julius. He took a deep breath and stepped up to the doctor with the all the confidence he could muster. Despite being a wealthy, prominent business man in Frankfurt for most of his adult life, all he had to offer was a broken-down body, ravaged by the harsh treatment at Buchenwald.

The doctor looked at Julius and realized immediately he wasn't in the best of shape. There were others who had passed before him who had suffered under the Nazis. He was used to looking into eyes filled with fear, pain, and desperation. Whether it was compassion, hatred for Hitler or standing orders for the day that motivated him, the doctor smiled, stamped the visa as approved and said, "Welcome to America, Mr. Sommer."

"He made it!" Walter said to himself. Nothing could stop them now. He was going to the land of George Washington, Thomas Jefferson, and Benjamin Franklin. He had studied the American founding fathers with the dedication of a Yankee scholar. He was about to embark on the long-sought adventure to become an American!

Julius and Helen were in tears as they boarded the train that would take them to the Dutch border. Battered, impoverished, and forced to leave the country, they were delivered from the darkness that was descending on Germany. It broke Julius's heart to leave his brothers and sisters behind, but he was doing what was right for his family. He had first-hand knowledge of how Jews were treated in the concentration camps. He didn't think it was possible for human beings to act with such cruelty. Not only that, but it was Germans hurting Germans.

Though both Helen and Julius were exited, they still feared something could go wrong before they reached the border. The train was filled with SA, SS and Wehrmacht regulars. Anything could happen before they reached the Netherlands. They wouldn't relax until they were standing on

Dutch soil. Walter was oblivious to his parents anxiety. He was beginning the adventure of his lifetime.

The locomotive slowed down as the train approached a small border town. They were almost free. As the train was coming to a stop, an intimidating SS Colonel stepped into the car and walked directly toward Julius. Both Julius and Helen were terrified. They could still be arrested without cause. They were trembling as he asked for their exit papers. They handed him the visas and waited anxiously while he studied them. The Colonel pursed his lips and shook his head. "It's a shame nice German people like you have to leave the country, Mr. Sommer. Maybe things will get better someday. Much success in America," he wished them and then walked out of the car. Five minutes later the Sommer family recached the safety of Dutch soil. Walter's plans and persistence had paid off. They were on the way to America.

Voyage to America

JULIUS SOMERS HAD ENOUGH MONEY to book third class passage on the aging Dutch ocean liner, the SS Veendam out of Rotterdam. The Veendam also had a large cargo hold, which allowed the family's personal belongings to come with them. This was a necessity due to the fact that the Nazi's had confiscated all Julius's cash money. The furniture, jewelry and silver would need to be sold when they reached America in order to have money to live on until employment could be secured.

The Veendam, which made 15 knots at best, had a broken screw (propeller) and could only make half that speed for the journey. Despite the slow ride and rough winter seas, Walter looked at the trip as a quest like in the movies. He was realizing his dream of going to America.

During the day Walter roamed the ship and conversed with anyone who would speak English with him. He wanted to practice using the language of his new country. He found a man who claimed to be a college professor. When Walter bragged that he had studied about the United States in school. The professor asked Walter to prove it and 0ffered him a quarter if he could name the capital of Wisconsin. Walter smiled and eagerly answered. "Madison." The professor was a man of his word and handed him a silver quarter with the image of George Washington on it. Walter knew all about the Father of his new country. He had studied about America's founding fathers after watching his first American movie. It was a musical staring Shirley Temple. Walter started watching every American movie he could. He especially enjoyed the Cowboy and Indian westerns that Hollywood pumped out on a weekly basis. Walter was infatuated with the American movies to the point that during Fasching, a German holiday similar to Halloween, Walter dressed up as an American Indian one year and a cowboy the next. After seeing his beloved Germany become a living nightmare for the entire Jewish population, he was ready to start his life. In some ways he looked at the United States as Utopia; a place where a young man could accomplish anything as long as he was willing to work hard. After his strict German upbringing, hard work would never be an issue for Walter.

SS Veendam

The SS Veendam was part of the Holland America Line and was used primarily for the Rotterdam to New York Route. Her Maiden voyage took place on March 20, 1923. She was 576 feet long with a gross tonnage of 15,500 tons. Before the outbreak of World War II, the Veendam was primarily used to by families fleeing from the Nazi threat. After the outbreak of War, the ship continued to make the New York run until May of 1940 when she was captured by the Germans during the battle of the Netherlands. On September 17, 1939, while on her North Atlantic run, the Veendam rescued British sailors from the carrier HMS Courageous after she was sunk by a German U-boat. The ship was moved to Hamburg where it was converted into an accommodation ship for off duty U-boat crews. In 1943 the Veendam was repeatedly bombed by Allied planes but refused to sink. She was taken back by the Allies during the capture of Hamburg on May 4, 1945. After the end of World War II, the ship was taken to Rotterdam where it was used as an accommodation ship for returning Dutch crews. Soon afterwards the ship was returned to the Holland America line. The ship was in bad shape. It was partially submerged and had suffered heavy fire damage from the repeated bombings.

The Veendam was towed back to Amsterdam for repairs and continued operations as an ocean liner in 1947. She continued to ferry post war immigrants between Europe and North America until 1953. On October 30, 1953, the Veendam concluded her final voyage with 600 passengers to New York. She sailed to Baltimore under her own power and was scrapped in November 15,1953

As the Veendam crossed the Atlantic, there were plenty of reminders of what he had left behind. While most of the Jewish families, who had left everything behind traveled in third class, Nazi party officials aboard sat at the Captain's table and drank Champagne. Even on a Dutch ship in international waters, the Nazis still seemed to hold a place of privilege. Walter told himself that things would be different in America.

After sixteen days, Walter's heart began to race when he first saw the New York City skyline on the western horizon. For the last several years America was a mythical place where a person could pursue anything he wanted without fear of losing everything for being Jewish. He recognized the Empire State Building and the Chrysler Building. Those buildings were real. America was real! Tears filled Walter's eyes as the ship maneuvered into the Hudson River and he got his first glimpse of the Statue of Liberty. "I don't think Americans realize what that statue means to immigrants when they first arrive. It was like she was welcoming me personally to my new home. I was so overcome with the Statue of Liberty; all I could say was—Halleluiah!"

Unfortunately, when the ship reached Hoboken, New Jersey, the US Custom official greeted the Nazis on the ship like long-lost relatives, while treating the Jewish immigrants with the same disdain they endured in Germany. While the Nazis were passed through immigration without delay, the Sommer family was stopped and interrogated. The first question the customs officer asked was, "Are you a member of the Communist Party?" The second was, "Have you ever been involved in a plot to overthrow the government of Adolf Hitler." So much for the warm welcome Walter was expecting. Regardless of the rough beginning, Walter and his family had defied the odds and made it to America. Walter began his new life with only the quarter he earned from professor in his pocket. He considered himself lucky.

Welcome to New York

THE SOMMER FAMILY TOOK A cab to the Hoboken, New Jersey address given in the letter from Mr. Stern. As promised, the Sterns welcomed them to America and served a fine American meal. After a night of pleasant conversation, they slept in the guestrooms and left for New York City in the morning. "People thought it was cruel that the Sterns didn't help us out more, but that wasn't the case," Walter explained. "They were struggling to get by as best they could and couldn't afford to help us. We were grateful that they to sponsored us. Without their help, we would never have made it to safety.

With the small amount of cash he had with him, Julius Sommer took his family across the Hudson River and paid fifty dollars a month for a walk-up apartment in the Washington Heights neighborhood of Manhattan. As soon as they were settled, Julius began selling the family's household goods to raise enough money to live on.

Walter Hits American Ground Running

Water was determined not to be a burden on his family, so he immediately began to look for work. He learned through acquaintances from Frankfurt that a local garment company, French Fabrics, had hired German-Jewish immigrants and decided it would be a good place to start his job search. Walter used the quarter he earned on the ship for subway fare to the garment district. Eventually he found 135 Madison Avenue, paused for a moment, took a deep breath, then walked through the door determined not to leave without the job. The interview went well, but the owner, Mr. Kates, said he didn't have any positions open. The United States was still in the midst of the Great Depression and the unemployment rate was very high at the time. The company owner liked Walter and told him to stick around until noon and he would take him to lunch for his trouble. Walter accepted and asked if he could look around the factory. The owner agreed and told Walter to meet him back at his office in an hour.

As Walter walked through the factory he saw several areas that were in his opinion, not operating efficiently. He formulated a plan to pitch to Mr. Kates over lunch. Walter explained several things he could do that would increase company sales which would pay for his salary. "The work area wasn't organized and wasn't appealing to potential customers. I told them I could organize a small area for a showroom" Walter also suggested making sample books out of fabric remnants for the company's salesman. These fabrics were being thrown away at the time. He also pointed out that the end of the roll fabrics, which were given to a company in Brooklyn to make doll clothes could be sold out of the country. Walter proposed to sell those remnants to his Central American clients he had developed during his apprenticeship in Germany, explaining not only that he spoke Spanish, but he could type the language as well. By the time lunch was finished, Walter had a free meal and a new job. Amazingly, he had only been in the United States for three days. His salary was eleven dollars a week.

Walter gave most of his salary to his parents help with the bills. Finding it difficult to get their savings from the Swiss Banks, they sold their furniture, silver, linen and China. Anything of value was sold. Eventually, Helen secured a job as a seamstress at a glove factory. Julius, however, was having a difficult time. "My father still hadn't recovered physically from his time at concentration camp," Walter said. "He was very weak and what made things worse was he didn't speak any English. My mother could speak some English and was able to converse with some of our neighbors. My father didn't understand a word and began to feel isolated. He also was heartbroken when he learned that Americans bought their coffee pre-roasted in cans. He had intended to open up a coffee store much like Wittwe Hassan in Frankfurt, but soon realized the formula wouldn't work in America."

Now gainfully employed Walter was eager to fit in as a local. However, making American friends wasn't easy. "Times were tough, and unemployment was high. People looked at us as refugees who were taking their jobs. I had to take the subway to work and after a few days, I met a couple of young people who were friendly. We made a point of sitting together until one day they told me they weren't allowed to talk to me anymore. When I asked why, they said it was because I was a refugee." Walter found himself feeling like a second-class citizen once again.

The difference was that in America, he could do something about it. "When I looked in the mirror, I still had my German clothes and I did indeed look like an immigrant," Walter lamented. "So I got an advance on my salary and bought an American suit for twenty-five dollars." Walter bragged that he got it wholesale and paid half price. Two weeks later, he got rid of his German shoes and replaced them with wingtips. Finally, he looked like a New Yorker.

Walter's first American friends

A couple of weeks later Walter stepped out of his apartment and heard unfamiliar music coming from the upstairs apartment. "It was the most beautiful music I had ever heard. It didn't sound like the heavy music from German composers such as Bach, Beethoven, and Wagner. It was light and cheerful. I followed the music and found myself knocking on a stranger's door. A young woman and man opened the door and invited me inside. They told me the music was by a Russian named Tchaikovsky. I was surprised to learn that the music was almost a hundred years old. But then again, anything Russian was outlawed in Nazi Germany. They were students at the City College of New York, Eventually, I learned that they were card carrying members of the American Communist Party. As a German I was taught to hate the Bolsheviks. But, they were nice to me, so I didn't care about their politics. They were my first American friends."

"They thought that Joseph Stalin was the greatest statesman in the history of the world. I'd been trained to believe that the godless Communists were the natural born enemy of all Germans. Regardless of their political views, they were the first New Yorkers to be kind to me. Over the next few years, we became very good friends. They taught me about the United States, and I tried to convince them that Communism wasn't so good." During his first summer in America, Walter talked them into joining the American Youth Hostel with him. The AYH was a Christian organization whose purpose was to get young people out of the city and into the country. It was Walter's first look at America outside of New York City. "I enjoyed every minute of it," Walter explained. "We biked out of the city and slept in barns and bunkhouses. We did chores for the farmer for food and board. After a day or two we'd move on to another farm. It was a great experience."

Walter also met new people when the family joined a small progressive synagogue in Manhattan. "There were only a handful of families in the congregation with a total membership of 100 people. It was a place that made us feel at home. We looked at other temples, but we didn't have enough money to join. We found the right place for the family."

Walter also remembers the efforts of Riverside Church near Columbia University. "Someone from the church invited me to come to a diner party. Not only did they invite me, but they told me to bring as many Jewish immigrants as I could. They said they realized that the Jews fleeing Germany hadn't been accepted with open arms. They wanted to make amends and did their best to welcome us to New York. Besides family dinners, they also threw mixers for young people. It was a great way to make new friends. It was also a wonderful way for me to meet girls. Everyone else was saying we don't want any immigrants. Part of the problem was that we all wore German clothing. People would say, 'there go all the German immigrants They want our jobs.' In the beginning, New York was not a friendly place. But, we had no place else to go.

As much as Walter liked socializing, he liked making money even more. Walter looked for other ways to earn income in his afterwork hours and on the weekends. He met a man who sold plastic shower curtains in bright colors. "He gave me a box full of the curtains and I sold them door to in the apartment buildings," Walter explained. "The curtains sold for four dollars, and I got to keep a dollar from everyone I sold. I also got a job working Saturdays at a gas station. I pumped gas and checked under the hood for ten cents an hour and I got to keep the tips. The money from my full-time job went to the family to help with the bills. The money I made on the part-time jobs allowed me to get a sandwich, watch a movie or go on a date."

Walter soon learned that dating a girl in New York could get expensive. After getting settled into his American life, he found American girls to be different than German girls. "I couldn't afford an American girlfriend," he laughed. "Girls from the United States wanted to be taken out for a nice meal. With a salary of eleven dollars a week I just couldn't afford it. An immigrant girl was happy to split a coke or a milkshake at a dime store. The most I could afford to spend on a date was a quarter, so I was limited to foreign girls."

One of those girls was named Mary Kleinman. She came from a prominent family in Vienna, Austria. Walter went on to say that Austrian girls were also expensive to date, but still much cheaper than the Americans. "The mothers of immigrant girls often threw social parties on the weekend which worked out well, because they didn't cost anything. Mary's, mother threw parties every Saturday afternoon. We would eat cake and punch and then read German literature. After that we would listen to German music. It was like the parties we used to have in Frankfurt. After the party we would go to a movie. Movies were only a dime, so they were good for a cheap date. I watched a lot of movies back in those days and I rarely went alone," Walter joked. Walter like musicals and romantic comedies. He remembers the quirky blonde bombshell Betty Hutton as one of his favorites.

Walter encounters Discrimination in America at Home

Walter also spent a lot of time with a girl named Maria, a Puerto Rican artist from work. We used to go horseback riding in Central Park on Sunday mornings. Normally it cost three dollars to ride, but on Sunday mornings during church hours, it only cost a quarter. "We spent a lot of time together, but in the end my mother didn't approve of me seeing a girl from the islands. After a year, I brought Maria to meet my parents. My mother took one look at her permanent sun tan and immediately said that our family had an important previous engagement that she had forgotten to tell me about. She told me to take Maria to the nearest train station and give her fare to get home. Maria was very understanding, but she knew the story about the prior plans wasn't true. My father was more open minded, but my mother wanted me to be with a nice German girl. She was too set in her ways. We saw each other for another six months, but I never took her home with me again. Everybody has prejudices," Walter sighed. "As far as my mother was concerned, only a nice German Jewish girl would be accepted."

Walter was very sensitive when it comes to pre-conceived prejudices. After suffering so much under the Nazi regime for being Jewish, he had a hard time accepting his mother judging this girl by the color of her skin. "We are all just people," Walter said. "Nobody is better than anybody else." In the end the relationship was doomed to fail. Walter's strict up-bringing would not let him defy his mother.

In 1940, Walter took a bus trip to Florida to visit some family friends and encountered systematic racism in America for the first time. "I had heard about racism in the south, but it broke my heart when I saw it firsthand. I first noticed the difference when African American passengers were forced to sit in the back of the bus. It reminded me of how I was treated in Germany after 1933. I could look in their faces and I knew exactly what they were thinking. To be treated that way makes you feel like your less of a person. Nobody should have to feel that way." Walter recounted the bus stops where restrooms and water fountains were segregated. "Only white people could eat at the lunch counters. The African Americans had to get their food from a walk-up window in the back of the restaurant. The worst thing about the whole trip occurred when I had to transfer to another bus in North Carolina," Walter recounted. "When the bus stopped, an entire African American family was forced to leave the bus so I could have my seat. I thought I had seen the last of that type of behavior in Germany. I never expected things to be like that in America." Walter would remember this incident and vowed to do something about discrimination if he ever got the chance.

Walter thrived in his new country due to his desire to better himself and the freedom to do so. His father, Julius, struggled to do the same.

Julius, who had been a successful entrepreneur in Germany, didn't know what to do with himself in America. Walter tried to teach him English but at 53 years of age, he struggled. However, after taking a tour of the glove factory where Helen was a seamstress, Julius realized he had the skills necessary to cut gloves from the rolls of raw leather and took a job with the company.

Julius and Helen in New York

It was while his parents were working at the glove factory that Walter's sister, Lore, befriended the daughter of the company's owner, a German girl by the name of Louise Levite. When she was introduced to Walter, he immediately became smitten with her. Unfortunately, Louise was only sixteen and Walter was twenty-one, so they were unable to date. That being said, Walter kept his eye on the dark-haired girl from Bavaria. Louise liked Walter but had several boyfriends who were of the appropriate age.

One day at work someone told Walter he should get a high school degree, so he applied to George Washington High School in Manhattan. After taking the entrance exam, the school told he that he was so advanced in his studies that they couldn't teach him a thing. They had him take a course in American History and a course on the constitution. As soon as the classes were completed. Walter was given his High School Diploma. Walter was thrilled to get his degree from such a prestigious school. Former Secretary of State Henry Kissinger was an underclassmen at George Washington at the time of his graduation. After graduation Walter enrolled at City College in New York. "I could already speak English, but I wanted to talk and write like an American, so I took speech and writing classes to help me lose my German accent."

When war broke out in Europe in September of 1939, Walter's thoughts went back to the family members who had been left back in Germany. Most of his aunts, uncles and cousins were still living under the heavy boot of the Nazis. It seemed unthinkable that Europe would fall back into another war only twenty years after World War I. Now that war had been declared, Hitler no longer had to worry about the world's perception of his anti-Jewish policies. It wasn't long before the Sommer family stopped receiving letters from their German relatives. They knew things were bad and were extremely worried, but didn't know just how dire the situation actually was. As Poland, The Netherlands, Czechoslovakia, Belgium, and finally France fell to Hitler's Army, they began to fear for the lives of their family members. They kept waiting for the United States to get into the war, but President Roosevelt continued to follow a policy of isolationism. To Walter it seemed like America was going to stand by and let all of Europe fall to the Nazis. Everyone was in limbo until an urgent message came over the radio. The date was December 7,1941.

"Our family was counting the days until America got into the war," Walter explained. There wasn't any question whether Walter would enlist or not. Serving in the Army had been a Sommer's family tradition for generations. It was considered a duty to fight for their country. The main difference in Walter's situation was that the Sommer's family had always fought on the side of Germany and Prussia before that; Walter would be fighting against Germany. When asked if he would be able to fight against the country that he loved, Walter sighed and almost reluctantly said he was okay with it. "The Germany of Hitler and the Nazis was no longer the Germany of my youth." The family believed that the sooner the Americans entered the war, the sooner Germany would be free from Adolf Hitler.

> *December 7, 1941—a date which will live in infamy—the United States of America was suddenly and deliberately attacked.*
>
> —Franklin D. Roosevelt

Pearl Harbor

IT WAS A COLD BLUSTERY afternoon in Manhattan and Walter was roller skating with his girlfriend on Lexington Ave and 57th Street when the music suddenly stopped. A voice came across the public address system and announced that Japan had just attacked Pearl Harbor. "You could have heard a pin drop in the rink," Walter remembered. "The announcer said that the rink would be closing in twenty minutes and that all members of the military were to report to their units immediately. December 7, 1941, changed everything. Everyone was angry. It was a cowardly attack. Everyone in New York City had their ear glued to the radio that day. Japan didn't stop at Pearl Harbor. They also attacked The Philippines, Malaysia, Hong Kong, Wake Island, Guam, Midway, Shanghai, and Thailand.

"That night we all listened to President Roosevelt's Day of Infamy speech. It was a shock to say the least," Walter said. War was declared around midnight. The other shoe dropped when Adolf Hitler declared war on the United States three days later. There was a good chance Walter would be fighting against his beloved Germany. "New Yorkers were shocked when Hitler declared war on the United States," Walter explained. "There were lots of pro German people who thought Hitler was a great guy. I wasn't one of those people. I didn't have any qualms about fighting my old country. The Nazis were evil and needed to be eliminated. It had to be done. The men in my family had always answered the call. My parents were worried about my well-being, but they never tried to stop me from doing my duty."

Walter along with thousands of young men went to the recruitment office to enlist. On December 8,1941. He was eager and feeling patriotic toward his new country. After waiting in line for hours, a burly Sargent called his name. Walter took a seat and handed his identification papers to the man. The Sargent began laughing. "These papers say that you're German, Mr. Sommer. You're in the wrong Army, Adolf," he told him. Despite Walter's explanation that he was a loyal American, he was classified as an Enemy Alien. Walter was devastated. Once again, Walter was rejected by his country. Only this time instead of Germany rejecting him for being Jewish, America was rejecting him for being German. He couldn't help but see the irony in it all. Walter soon learned that irony can be fickle.

On January 29, 1942, Walter received his draft notice. Enemy alien or not, Uncle Sam wanted him to serve after all. When he reported at the draft office, he was sent to the same Sargent who had called him Adolf on the day he tried to enlist. The Sargent recognized Walter and shook his head in disbelief. "Oh well," he said. "Uncle Sam welcomes you to the Army."

Walter at Ft Bragg

A few weeks later Walter reported to Fort Dix, New Jersey and was sworn into the Army. At Fort Dix the recruits were asked if they finished high school. Only twenty five percent had diplomas. At that point he volunteered for artillery and was chosen. Walter had come from a long line of artillery men in Germany dating back for nearly a century. When asked if he wanted to carry on in the family tradition, Walter began to laugh before answering. "Heavens no," he replied "I volunteered for the artillery because I didn't want to be assigned to the infantry. Everybody knew you had a better chance of getting killed in the infantry. Rule number one was do whatever you can to stay alive. When they found out I knew trigonometry. I was a shoe-in. I was sent to Fort Bragg, North Carolina for gunnery school.

After a few days Walter's intellect became apparent and he was brought to the attention of the Company Commander. Because of his education, Walter was seen as officer material. It was decided he would be more valuable to the Army as a second lieutenant and was sent to Officer Training School. After two months Walter was excelling when his commanding officer called him into his office. "Private Sommer, what in the hell do you think you're doing? You didn't you tell us you weren't an American citizen." the officer growled. "Not only that, but you are also an enemy alien! Why didn't you tell us?"

"Because nobody asked me," Walter replied. "I was just following orders." Walter defended himself by saying that his drill instructor had emphasized that he was to follow orders and not ask questions. "So I didn't ask questions. They immediately sent me back to artillery school as a private. I was destined to serve as a simple enlisted soldier."

After finishing gunnery school at Fort Bragg, Walter was assigned to Battery A, 306 Field Artillery Battalion of the 77th Infantry Division. Since the 77th was from New York City, they were known as the Statue of Liberty Division. Ironically, It was the 77th Infantry Division that stopped the German Army from taking Paris in World War I. "My parents were so sure that Germany was going to win World War I, my mother made a Victory Quilt to celebrate the occasion. Things changed when the Americans in general, and the 77th in particular, joined the war. My uncles fought against the 77th and twenty years later I was a member of the Statue of Liberty Brigade, the very division that won the war for the allies.

77th Infantry Division Patch

After graduating from artillery school, Walter's battalion was sent to the swamps of East Texas for mud training. "It was a miserable place," Walter recalled. "It was hot and humid, and the mosquitos seemed to be as big as birds. We all complained, but we learned how to move our cannon in two feet of mud. Later on this was imperative when we were on the jungle islands in the Pacific."

"After swamp training in the winter of 1943 we were moved to West Virginia. Since we didn't know whether we were going to be sent to the European or Pacific Theatre, we had to train for every contingency," Walter explained. "This time we had to learn to operate our artillery in snow in the mountains. It was as cold in West Virginia as it had been hot in Texas. Both places were miserable, but we were coming together as a well-trained unit. We were ready to get into the war, but the Army decided we needed more training. This time we were headed to the desert."

"We loaded our cannons onto a train and started off for Arizona. Five hundred miles into the trip, the locomotive broke down in the Western Indiana town of Terre Haute," Walter said. "The temperature was below freezing and there was six inches of snow on the ground. I was ordered to guard the Howitzers on the flat car while the others got to stay on the train or get something to eat at a nearby restaurant. Needless to say, I was not happy about drawing guard duty on such a cold day. I had only been there a few minutes when a group of local people showed up with hot coffee and donuts. Not only did it help keep me warm, but it also left me with a fond feeling for the people of Terre Haute. As things turned out that experience helped me years later when it came time to make one of the most important decisions in my life."

Two days later the battalion made camp outside of Phoenix, Arizona. "The desert was barren, but it was a nice change from the cold and snow we left behind," Walter remembered. "We set up camp in the middle of nowhere and fired a lot of ammunition at lizards and rattlesnakes. By this time, we were well trained and spent a lot of time doing nothing. In the Army, it always seemed to be hurry up and wait. The scuttlebutt around camp said that we were going to ship out any day. As usual, the scuttlebutt was wrong. Every day the war continued while we were still in the States. It was hard to take. We wanted to get in the fight. Of course we didn't know what war looked like, but we thought we were ready. Looking back now, I realize how naïve we actually were."

Training in Arizona

"In Arizona we spent a lot of time fighting boredom," Walter explained. "One bright spot was receiving passes to go into Phoenix on the weekend. We didn't have enough money for a hotel room, so we pitched pup tents at the edge of the city in the desert. Several churches held dances and mixers for the soldiers to keep us out of the bars. They would serve sandwiches, cookies, and punch. It was good clean fun. At one of these dances I met a nice Christian girl by the name of Georgia Koontz. We hit it off from the beginning and started seeing each other every weekend. Eventually, we fell in love, and I promised to return to her after the war." Walter sighed. "I didn't keep my promise. I ended up marrying the right girl for me, but I have always felt bad about breaking Georgia's heart."

Walter and Georgia Koontz in Phoenix

"Things started to pick up after New Year's Day 1944," Walter said. "We loaded the cannons and the rest of our equipment onto trains to be shipped to the west coast. We would be headed for Hawaii in a matter of days. As the time drew closer, I got called into the Company Commander's office."

"Private Sommer. It has come to my attention that you are not an American citizen," the Commander growled. "Do you know what kind of Hell there would be to pay it I sent an enemy alien into battle? Why didn't you say something?"

"Nobody asked me," Walter replied. An hour later Walter was on an overnight train to Los Angeles accompanied by a Sargent and First Lieutenant. At ten o'clock the next morning Walter was stood before a judge in the Los Angeles Federal Court taking the Oath of Allegiance to the United States of America.

Before declaring him an American, the judge looked at Walter and declared the need to Americanize his name. "Private Sommer. In America we have an *s* on the end of our last names." He signed a paper, pounded his gavel, and declared that Walter Sommer, an enemy alien from Germany, was now Walter Sommers, an American citizen.

"It was still late morning when we reached the train station and found out that our train back to Arizona didn't leave until midnight," Walter recalled. "We had twelve hours to kill and not much money to spend. That's when I picked up a newspaper and read an article about German Nobel Prize winning author Thomas Mann who was living in exile in Malibu. I had read two of Mann's books and thought that he might enjoy talking to a fellow German who had also fled the country. I asked the Lieutenant for permission to call Mr. Mann and see if we might visit him. He thought I was crazy but said I could if I wanted."

"I contacted the operator and amazingly his number was listed. Mr. Mann answered the phone and when I explained our situation, he invited the three of us to his ocean front home for the afternoon. He served us cake, tea, and cucumber sandwiches. We talked about how Germany had changed under Adolf Hitler, and he said he hoped to go back some day when things got better. I told him that I would stay on this side of the Atlantic. I was an American now with no intention of turning my back on my new country. After a wonderful day, he wished us well and we took a cab back to the train station. A few hours later, we were on our way back to the Arizona desert. It was quite a day to remember. I had become an American citizen in the morning and spent the afternoon with a Nobel Prize winner. It doesn't get much better than that. A few days later we were sailing for Hawaii. The war was about to become a reality."

June 6, 1875- August 12, 1955, Paul Thomas Mann was a German novelist, short story writer, social critic, and the 1929 Nobel Prize in Literature laureate. His novels and novellas are known for their insight into the psychology of the artist and the intellectual. He was forced to leave Germany due to his criticism of the Nazi Regime and immigrated to Czechoslovakia in 1936. In 1939 when the Germans invaded Czechoslovakia, Mann moved to the United States. The outbreak of World War II on September 1, 1939 prompted Mann to offer anti-Nazi speeches to the German people via the BBC. In October 1940 he began monthly broadcasts, recorded in the U.S. and flown to London, where the BBC broadcast them to Germany. During these eight-minute addresses, Mann condemned Hitler and his henchmen as crude philistines completely out of touch with European culture. In one speech he said, "The war is horrible, but it has the advantage of keeping Hitler from making speeches about culture." Mann was one of the few publicly active opponents of Nazism among German expatriates in the U.S.

Thomas Mann

Pearl Harbor

On March 31, 1944, Walter and the 77th Infantry Division landed in Hawaii to continue amphibious training and learn jungle warfare. "We had been training for nearly two years and the officers had prepared us for the horrors of war, but everything became all too real when we sailed into Pearl Harbor and saw the sunken remains of the Battleship USS Arizona and results of the carnage. It seemed unbelievable that there were still over 1100 bodies entombed in the ship. That's when we realized how ruthless our enemy could be."

Despite the damage at Pearl Harbor, Walter was taken aback by the natural beauty of the Hawaiian Islands. "It was truly a paradise," he marveled. "Unfortunately, we drove right past the resorts and made camp forty miles outside of Honolulu. We set up at the edge of a remote jungle and began preparing for jungle warfare. It was part paradise and part hell. We didn't realize it at the time, but they were preparing us for the tropical islands in the Pacific that had to be taken on the road to Tokyo."

During this final phase of training the Army wanted the soldiers to get used to maneuvering while under live fire. "We had to crawl through trenches and under barbed-wire while machine guns fired live rounds only a few feet above our heads," Walter recalled. "I thought I was ready for battle, but I was wrong. I had never been so scared in my life. I was terrified but managed to work through it. That experience really paid off when we were under fire from the Japanese."

After a couple of days of hard work, a Sergeant asked for volunteers who knew how to drive a 6 x 6 Army truck. Thinking anything would be better than toiling in the hot sun, Walter immediately volunteered to drive the huge truck. The only problem was that Walter had never driven a truck in his life. "My father told me that I should use my time in the Army to learn new skills," Walter explained. Unfortunately, the Sergeant wasn't too impressed with Walter's reasoning. "He was mad as a hornet and told me I had twelve hours to become an expert driver. He didn't say what he would do to me if I didn't pass muster, but he made it clear it wouldn't be pleasant. I didn't sleep at all that night as I drove back and forth across the camp grinding gears and killing the engine in a way that made my lack of skills apparent to everybody around." But despite his lack of experience, Walter improved enough by morning to get the job. He was now in charge of the Battalion's commissary. The fact that he could type and had merchandising experience didn't hurt. One of his job duties was to drive to Honolulu twice a week for food and supplies. "It was wonderful duty," Walter remembered. "I was a very popular soldier when I returned. It gave me a break from marching and drills. We didn't know where we were going but they told us it would be jungle just like the one where we were training."

After a month of repetitive training, Walter recalled that the everybody was tired of the routine and ready for action. "We were well trained and ready to get into the war. Of course, since nobody had actually been in battle yet, we didn't really know what was instore for us. But that didn't matter. We were ready to fight."

"Late in March of 1944 rumors began to spread that we would be shipping out soon. Finally, the word came, and we were told to report to Pearl Harbor on a Sunday, We were all given a pass into town on the preceding Friday." While most of the men got off the shuttle bus at Oahu's Red-Light District with intentions of frequenting the brothels, bars, and tattoo parlors, Walter chose to continue on to Pearl Harbor. "I saw nothing but the trouble my buddies were going to get into, so I decided to explore the damage done at Pearl Harbor." Though the surprise attack had occurred two years prior, there was still a great deal of evidence of that fateful day. Walter was moved by the sight of the sunken USS Arizona as oil and diesel continued to seep into the harbor with over eleven hundred bodies buried inside. Despite the death and devastation he had witnessed under the Nazi regime it still amazed him just how cruel people could be toward each other. "Those men were sleeping in their bunks or getting ready for church when they were attacked," Walter explained with moistened eyes. "We weren't at war when the bombs fell and now they are resting in those bunks for eternity. It made it crystal clear that we were fighting on the right side of history."

As Walter walked around the base, he happened to come upon a giant US Navy PBY Catalina Flying Boat. "It was absolutely the biggest airplane I had ever seen. The wingspan was over a 100 feet. I had never flown on an airplane and wondered what it would be like to fly in such a magnificent machine. I saw a sailor loading equipment into the plane and asked what it would take to get a ride on the plane. The Sailor pointed toward a young Lieutenant who was walking toward them."

"Ask him. He's the pilot," he said and walked away.

So in his typical innocent demeaner, Walter explained to the pilot that he was on leave and was curious about the plane and asked if they allowed passengers on the mission. The Lieutenant thought about it for a moment, shrugged his shoulders and told him to throw on a flight suit. It is unknown how many military rules were broken as the little Army Corporal with the German accent, who had only been an American citizen for 120 days, flew on a five-hour mission hunting for Japanese submarines. Walter smiled as he remembered that day. "It was the thrill of a lifetime."

Walter In Leave in Hawaii

The Invasion of Guam

WALTER, ALONG WITH THE OTHER members of Battery A, 306 Field Artillery Battalion of the 77th Infantry Division, waited anxiously for their first taste of action in the South Pacific. Walter and his fellow G.I.s left Honolulu on a Merchant Marine Victory Ship on July 1, 1944. They knew they were headed for battle, but not where or when it would be. "Once we got into the Ocean, the convoy began to zig-zag to avoid Japanese submarines, so we didn't have any idea whether we were heading North, South, East or West," Walter explained. "We didn't know where we were going, so we could have been anywhere. They kept us in the dark so that if we were captured, we couldn't give away vital information. We heard rumors that we were headed towards the Mariana Islands. There was heavy fighting on Saipan, and it was unclear whether the 77th Division would be needed to help capture the island. Halfway to the Marianas, Saipan came under American control and 77th was attached to the 3rd Marine Division. The target was Guam, the first populated American territory to be captured from the Japanese."

"They told us that we were going to Guam only two hours before landing," Walter remembered. "When we went to the briefing, I learned that I was on a team of four men going in with the first wave. It was our job to find a spot to deploy our 155mm Howitzers and prepare for the Battalion's arrival. Since there weren't enough LSTs to land everybody, we climbed over the side of the ship on a cargo net with all of our equipment. The Higgins Boats waiting for us were bouncing up and down with the waves as we jumped into the landing craft. It would have been hard enough under the best conditions, but I was carrying a pack weighing thirty pounds along with a thirty-five-pound radio. On top of that, I had my 30-caliber carbine along with a couple of hand grenades. I don't think I could have carried another thing."

Walter's heart pounded as the Higgins Boat made its way toward the beach as the Naval guns pummeled the islands interior. The noise was deafening. "I was well trained but untested under fire," he explained. "At this point I tried to put everything out of my mind and concentrate on my assignment." When the front of the boat opened up, Walter saw he was two hundred yards from the beach. It was low-tide, and the Higgins Boat couldn't clear the coral reef. Walter waded to the beach in waist-deep water. "I was expecting to come under fire immediately, but the Marines had cleared the beach and the Japanese had moved inland. There were both Marine and Japanese bodies on the beach. The War suddenly became real for me."

"We walked onto the beach, checked our maps and found our spot. We followed a path into the jungle, and I was immediately overcome by the stench of dead bodies. The battleships and cruisers had pounded the island for a week and there were body parts everywhere. To make matters worse, the humidity was high in the jungle and the temperature topped one hundred degrees. I covered my mouth and kept hiking toward our destination. After three miles we found a good spot to place our cannon. There were dozens of dead Japanese bodies scattered around the area. After radioing our position back to the ship, another corporal and I spent the next five hours burying body parts with our tiny trench shovels. It was absolutely the worst thing I saw during the war," Walter admitted. When finished with the gruesome detail, Walter dug a foxhole for protection through the night. Up until that point, Walter had not come under fire, but that would not last long. "As the sun went down the Japanese opened fire on us," Walter recalled. "They were experienced night fighters and fought like demons. We were out in the open and the only protection we had was the foxhole. Bullets were flying everywhere, and I soon learned the lesson that you couldn't dig a foxhole too deep. I didn't get a wink of sleep that first night. When daylight came, the infantry fortified their position and started pushing the Japanese toward the north side of the island."

That meant that Walter had to move up too. Even though the 155mm cannon was behind the front line, it was Walter's job, as a forward artillery spotter, to call back instructions from the front line. Walter was part of a three-man team consisting of a lieutenant, sergeant, and a corporal. Walter was the corporal. "I carried a pencil and paper along with a slide rule and a trigonometry formula book. It was my job to figure the formula and call back coordinates to the gun crews. Halfway through the Battle of Guam, I realized that the log tables provided by the Army were not as good as my high school trigonometry book from Frankfurt. I wrote to my mother and asked her to send my old German text book, which I used for the duration of the war. The Island of Guam was five miles wide and eighteen miles long and I must have walked every inch of it."

Walter At Mess Hall

"The lieutenant was supposed to double check my figures but soon learned to trust my work. It usually took three shots before I had the target locked in. The first shot would be long, the second shot short, and the third shot was deadly." Because the Japanese soldiers could sometimes hear radio messages, Walter's unit ran telephone lines back to the cannon. In the jungle, they used palm and coconut trees to hang the wire. One of Walter's duties was to climb the trees and hang the wire at the top. "I was one of the best at climbing the trees. It would have been fun if it were not for the fact that Japanese snipers would take shots while I was doing it."

The Battle of Guam started on July 21 and ended on August 10, 1944. Walter and the 77th infantry spent the next two months occupying the island awaiting their next assignment. Boredom soon set in. "Hurry up and wait," Walter laughed. "That's how it was in the Army. The food was okay for the most. We ate C and K rations and every now and then a mobile kitchen would show up and we would eat a hot meal."

One of Walter's most memorable incidents occurred when he received cans of corned beef from his mother. It was in between engagements when the meat arrived during mail call. "It was like receiving Manna from Heaven," Walter laughed. "We had been eating K rations, so it was a real treat. A buddy of mine managed to liberate a loaf of bread and some small cans of beer. We had a feast in the middle of a battle zone. It was nice to have a taste of home in the middle of all the death and destruction."

Betty Hutton Entertains the Troops

Walter often volunteered to drive to fight the boredom. "It gave me something to do and helped the day go quicker." Walter was ordered to go to the hospital on the south side of the island and return with a passenger, and all too happy to go. Word had reached the front line that a ship full of Marine nurses had arrived at the island. It had been weeks since any of the troops had even seen a woman. Besides that, the hospital served the best food on the island. It was a win/win situation. He headed south with high expectations but wasn't prepared for what then happened.

Upon arrival Walter was told to get something to eat and then wait with his jeep for his passenger. When his passenger showed up, he couldn't believe his eyes. It was his favorite Hollywood actress, Betty Hutton; he was assigned to drive her around Guam while she met and entertained the troops. "She was wonderful!" Walter exclaimed "She was a very nice girl. When I told her that I had never met a movie star, she laughed and told me, That's okay Walter, you are the first person I've ever met who was born in Germany."

Invasion of Leyte

AFTER SAILING AROUND THE SOUTH Pacific, Walter, and the G.I.s from the 77ᵗʰ Infantry got a reprieve from the boredom when their ship stopped at New Caledonia for some R & R (rest and recuperation.) "It was a tropical French Island with beautiful beaches. We swam in the ocean, had three good meals a day, and played baseball on the beach. There were plenty of hot dogs, cold beer, and Coca-Cola along with USO entertainment. After the fierce fighting on Guam, it was nice to get away from the war for a little bit." It gave Walter time to read and reflect on the letters from home. "We literally lived from mail call to mail call. Letters from family and friends really kept us going. Of all of the letters I received during the war, Louise's letters were by far the best."

Walter often read and wrote letters for illiterate soldiers. "It was sad that in a country like the United States that so many boys had never attended school and were illiterate," Walter said. "I hoped that the letters I wrote for the soldiers gave comfort to their families." These simple acts of kindness marked the beginning of a lifetime of helping others.

The reprieve from the war ended all too soon and Walter found himself on an LST bound for the Philippine island of Leyte, once again mired in boredom as the days of zigzagging across the South Pacific seemed endless. "We were packed into the ship like sardines and there wasn't anything to do. That suddenly changed one morning shortly after sunrise, when Walter was laying in his bunk and heard a boom in the front of the ship. "Nobody knew what had happened but then the ship started leaning to the starboard side," Walter recalled. "We had been bombed by a Japanese bomber, known as a Betty. We stood on deck for a while, until it became obvious that the ship was going to capsize. I remember sliding down the side as the ship listed at a 45-degree angle. We made our way to a Higgins Boat and then watched helplessly as the ship slowly slipped into the water. By the end of the day we were all assigned to nearby ships. So much for being bored. It wasn't long before we heard the thunder of the ships pounding an island in the distance. We had arrived at Leyte."

General Douglas MacArthur fulfills his 'I Shall Return' promise to the Filipino people as he wades ashoe at Red Beach on Leyte. Walter Sommers came ashore on the same beach one day earlier.

On October 20, 1944, Walter and the 77th Infantry landed on a Philippine beach under heavy Japanese gunfire. Having felt secure for the prior two months, Walter once again found himself taking cover on the beach as bullets flew overhead. "The Japanese were waiting for us, and we took several casualties during the landing," Walter explained. "Much like Guam, we were ordered to find a position to set up our cannon. Even though we were in a tropical climate, Leyte Island was quite different to Guam. Guam had been all jungle, where Leyte had a lot of open space without much cover. It required a lot more digging of trenches and foxholes. But it wasn't long before we had the Japanese retreating. Even when they retreated, the Japanese left snipers in the trees who didn't seem to care whether they lived or died. They would stay up there for days and shoot when we least expected it. It caused a lot of sleepless nights. We were all sleep deprived."

"As spotters we had to move forward whenever the front line advanced. When we established a new position, we ran telephone lines back to the cannon. We had to hang wire from coconut trees up to a distance of a half mile. Once again I became a target for the snipers every time I climbed one. After being shot at a couple of times I declined to volunteer for that duty."

An incident that haunted Walter after World War II occurred during the invasion of Leyte. When not serving as an artillery spotter, Walter was required to stand guard duty. One evening Walter was ordered to protect his unit while they slept. He was positioned in the back of a Jeep armed with a 50-caliber machine gun. "It was dark and hard to see," Walter recalled. 'There was a clearing in front of me, but everything beyond was jungle. We could hear the Japanese soldiers all through the night. They liked to keep us awake by yelling insults at us in English. We never knew when they were going to attack. Most nights nothing happened, but you still had to be ready. They made sure to let us know they were only a few yards away. Their job was to make sure we didn't get any sleep and they were good at their job."

As Walter struggled to see any sign of the enemy he noticed movement in the jungle. Someone was running for the camp. Walter called out for them to identify themselves. "I had to make sure he wasn't American before opening fire." Walter explained as a solemn expression came over his face. "When he didn't answer, I opened fire. I didn't think. I just did it. We were all well-prepared and my training simply took over. I had to protect my brothers." When the smoke cleared and everyone in the camp was alerted, we found the body of a very nice Japanese man only feet outside the camp perimeter. His body was wired with explosives as he was making a Bonsai charge. His mission was to blow himself up along with all of us. Miraculously the explosives did not go off." Walter had saved the lives of his unit.

Decades later, as he recalled this incident, I couldn't help but notice that Walter referred to the Japanese soldier as being a "very nice man." When I questioned him why he felt this way about a man who was trying to kill him and his comrades, I was surprised by his response. "When

Captain Weber searched the soldier's body, all he found was a picture of the man with his son. They were both smiling at the camera. That's when I realized that he wasn't all that different from me."

A few days later, Walter was on patrol with two other soldiers and as the sun was setting, they realized they were lost. Trying to study the map by the flame of a Zippo lighter, they heard footsteps approaching through the jungle. They took cover when they realized it was a Japanese patrol, and they were behind enemy lines. "It was one of the longest nights in my life," Walter explained. "After wandering around the jungle for hours we finally heard a group of men speaking in English. We called out and walked into their camp and were shocked to see every one of the soldiers were African American. The Army was still segregated. Black soldiers mostly served as cooks in mobile kitchens. We assumed that we had stumbled into one of these units. We were saved. They fed us a good meal and took us to a dark tent and pulled out cots for us to sleep on and told us they would feed us breakfast before we left in the morning. They couldn't have been any nicer to us. Little did we know that they had just played a practical joke on us."

"We were so tired, we slept like the dead," Walter laughed. With good reason. When the three soldiers awoke in the morning, they saw that their cots had been placed in a battlefield morgue occupied by several bodies. Besides being on mobile kitchen units, African Americans were also assigned to battlefield burial crews. "It was quite a fright," Walter remembered. "They got us good. I can't really blame them for having some fun at our expense. They had a lousy job but followed orders and did their duty. Soldiers did whatever they could to keep their sanity with so much death around them."

The practical joke also reminded Walter that his new country was far from perfect. Much like the time when a black family was forced to get off the bus to make room for him, these soldiers were relegated to serve as cooks or janitors or grave diggers. Just as it was in Germany, prejudice was prejudice.

The battle in Leyte continued until the end of March 1945. "There were still large pockets of resistance, and there were times when we would engage in combat and then rotate back behind the frontlines. There was a lot of down time and a lot of the fellas got bored. There was nothing to do," Walter recalled. "My old boss and some of my friends at French Fabrics used to send me dollar bills. It was a nice gesture but there wasn't anything or anyone to spend the money on. I wrote them back and asked them to send something useful. So about a month later I received a box filled with colorful cloth remnants. They were end pieces left over from rolls. When I took them to a nearby Philippine village, the women went crazy. They had never seen anything so bright and colorful. It started a local bidding war and at the end of the day I ended up trading the fabric for enough chickens and fixings to serve a chicken dinner to 100 soldiers in my unit. I was very popular that day."

Walter and Liway Castaneda

A few days later, Walter met a Jewish Philippine banana farmer who insisted that he spend time with the family. "His wife had made several dresses from the remnants I had traded. When they found out that I was Jewish, they invited me for dinner." Apparently his family had come to the Philippines when the Spanish first conquered the island in the 1500s. What I didn't realize was that he was looking for a husband for his daughter. Her name was Liway Castaneda. She was a very pretty girl, and we spent quite a bit of time together. I really liked her, and her father offered me my very own banana and coconut farm if I would marry her. It was a tempting offer, but I was writing to three girls back in the states. Georgia Koonce in Phoenix. Mary Kleinman in New York, along with my sister Lore's best friend Louise Levite. Besides, I could only imagine what my mother would do if I brought home a war bride from the Philippines. My mother was rooting for Louise Levite."

Okinawa

On April 15, 1945, Walter and the 77th headed for the Okinawan Island of Ie Shima for what Walter described as the most intense fighting he encountered during the war. Japanese considered Okinawa part of their homeland and were determined to fight to the death. In addition to conventional hazards, the 77th Infantry Division encountered *kamikaze* attacks against their ship while waiting to make their landing. Walter and the other artilleryman were actually given jobs to support the Navy gunners. They helped with the ammunition and trained to replace gunners if they became incapacitated. During one attack Walter played a role in shooting down a *kamikaze* plane.

"The fighting on Okinawa was horrible," Walter remembers, but this was our third battle. We were battle-hardened veterans. We all were good at our jobs and knew exactly what to do." During the landing and then again once they were on the island the 77th came under Kamikaze suicide attacks for the first time. "There wasn't any defense to the Kamikazes, but fortunately for me as a forward artillery spotter I was in a group of three men. We were much too small of a target. They looked for ships, tanks, or larger groups of soldiers. It was still hard to understand how these men committed suicide for their emperor."

Walter may have been immune to Kamikaze attacks, but as a front area spotter, Walter was in sight of the enemy who at the time occupied higher ground. "The snipers shot at us twenty-four hours a day and kept us pinned down in trenches and foxholes." Walter also ran into the heaviest artillery fire of the Pacific war. They were plastered day and night by field pieces of all sizes. The enemy's pillboxes were superior to any in use at Guam or Leyte.

"My job was mostly doing math problems to figure out firing solutions for the cannons, while keeping my head down. It was a hard-fought battle for every inch of ground." Over the two-day period they were engaged in a bitter fight for "Government House Hill" and "Bloody Ridge." They were considered some of the bloodiest fighting of the war.

World renowned journalist Ernie Pyle accompanied Walter and the 77th in landing at Ie Shima to record the agony of the American foot soldiers. On the morning of April 18, 1945, Pyle stopped by to talk to Walter and his unit as they were eating breakfast. "Ernie asked me how I was doing and if they were giving us enough to eat," Walter remembered. "I assured him that we were. 'He was our guy.' He was always looking out for us."

Two hours after talking with Walter, Ernie Pyle was killed by an enemy sniper.

Ernie Pyle Sharing Stories with the 77th

Ernie Pyle (August 3, 1900 – April 18, 1945) was a Pulitzer Prize winning American journalist and war correspondent best known for his stories about ordinary American soldiers during World War II. Pyle is also known for stories as a roving human-interest reporter from 1935 through 1941 about ordinary people.. When the United States entered World War II, he used his folksy style of human-interest stories to his wartime reports from Europe (1942–44) and the Pacific Theatre in 1945. Pyle won the Pulitzer Prize in 1944 for his newspaper accounts of the dogface infantry soldiers from a first-person perspective. He was killed by enemy fire on Iejima during the Battle of Okinawa.

On April 25 Ie Shima was declared secure enough to build an air field. Walter and the 77th next went to the main island of Okinawa to join the main invasion force. They remained in constant battle until June as Walter's unit constantly bombarded the Japanese troops that had gone to the caves, refusing to surrender. "It was a different kind of battle," Walter recalled. "The Japanese refused to surrender, even though everything was hopeless for them. I never felt comfortable any time I stuck my head up out of the foxhole."

Walter stayed on Okinawa until July when the 77th was sent to the Island of Cebu in the Philippines to prepare for the invasion of the Japanese mainland.

It should be noted that Japanese defense of Okinawa was so vicious and the casualties so high that it played a role in President Truman's decision to use the atomic bomb rather than commit to the invasion of the Japanese mainland.

Cebu

After weeks of training on Cebu Island in the Philippines with the 77th Infantry as they prepared for the final invasion of Japan, Walter recognized that the upcoming battle would likely be worse than anything they had experienced. "The Japanese considered Okinawa to be their soil and defended it to the death," Walter explained. "They fought like demons. Of the 120,000 Japanese troops on Okinawa only 8,000 survived. They would rather die than surrender. If they fought this hard for an island territory, how hard would they fight on Japanese soil? "Captain Weber warned us to be prepared for the invasion to end the war. He made it clear that many of us wouldn't be going home alive. Captain Weber had taken care of us from our training in the states through three island invasions. Up until then, he had said that our training would keep us alive. I could tell by the look on his face that it might not be the case during the invasion. Nevertheless, he prepared us in a way that would give us the skill we needed to have the best shot of survival. He was one of the best officers under whom I served. He cared about us. He was a good man."

"The guys in the unit joked around, but we all knew that there would be bad times ahead. You tried to tell yourself that it couldn't happen to you, but all you had to do was look for the missing faces to realize that wasn't true. We heard estimates that up to a million Americans could die during the Japanese invasion. I did the math and didn't like the odds," Walter laughed.

"Then on August 6, 1945, something happened that would change the world. A nuclear bomb called 'Little Boy' was dropped on the city of Hiroshima from the B-29 Superfortress Enola Gay flown by Colonel Paul Tibbets. We didn't know what an A-Bomb was or the extent of its destructive force. Even if we had known, it wouldn't have made any difference. The Empire of Japan surrendered after a second bomb was dropped on the City of Nagasaki. The war was over, and a million Americans didn't have to die. That night we had what had to be the party of the century. I have never been so drunk before or since. I didn't care. I had survived the war and would be going home in six months," Walter said and then the smile disappeared from his face. "We didn't get to celebrate long, when we woke up the next morning, with the world's worse hangovers, we learned that Captain Weber had killed himself during the night. In his note he explained that he had gotten a girl pregnant in Hawaii and because of that he knew he could never go home. He said that he wanted to do whatever he could to see his boys survive the war and now that he had accomplished his mission there was only one thing left to do."

Walter shook his head and looked away. "It was a very bad war," he whispered.

When I mentioned to Walter that most of the Word War II veterans I have met hate the Japanese because of their brutal tactics, I ask him why he didn't feel that way. He paused for a moment and replied "Hate is a word that is not in my book. We were at war. I had a job to do."

Walter first hears about the Concentration Camps in Europe

While waiting to leave for the occupation of Japan, Walter received a letter from his mother that was to foretell the horrible news about the fate of his remaining family in Germany. "Up until this point in the war, I had heard nothing about the death camps in Europe. We had been told that our family had been sent to work camps for the German war effort, but not a word of the Holocaust had made its way to the Pacific Theatre. She didn't say much but told me to prepare for the worst as the news trickled in a little at a time. It wasn't until a few months after the war that I learned just how bad things had been in Europe.

Time in Japan and The Beginning of the Cold War

WALTER ARRIVED AT THE ISLAND of Hokkaido, the northern most of the Japanese islands, shortly after the Japanese surrender. "We were told to be prepared for animosity, but in reality, the Japanese people couldn't have been any nicer. They were just happy that the war was finally over. The interesting part of our occupation on Hokkaido was that the Americans occupied the south end of the Island and Soviet troops occupied the northern end," Walter explained. "We were not heavily armed, and the Russians were armed to the teeth. We tried to talk to them, but they weren't allowed to talk to us." Walter went on to say that the Russians treated the Japanese people much more harshly than the Americans. "We were supposed to be allies with the Russians, but they acted more like enemies. I didn't realize it at the time, but I was witnessing the beginning of the Cold War."

Anyone who has met Walter Sommers soon realizes that he looks for the good in people. This was the case with the Japanese civilians he met on Hokkaido. "They invited me into their homes as soon as we arrived. It was discouraged at first, but then it was decided that it would be good for relations if the troops and the civilians were friendly. The first family I visited made a meal that was called stir fry. I had never seen anything like it. I don't know what was in it, but it sure was good." Walter explored the island taking time to learn as much as he could about the culture. "Somebody gave me a ticket to a Japanese play," Walter remembered. "They played strange music and I didn't understand a word they said, but I loved every minute of it."

222

Once Douglas MacArthur established his provisional government headquarters in Tokyo, it became necessary to form a bureaucracy to run the country. All soldiers in the Pacific Theatre with any clerical experience were recruited to Tokyo to deal with the massive amount of paperwork. Walter had already established himself as an expert typist and was sent to the capital city.

At the time Tokyo was the largest city in the world. Despite the damage done by years of bombing, it was a busy and intimidating city. Walter was assigned as clerk in an administration building and found it less friendly than Hokkaido. On one of his days off Walter, along with two other GIs, explored Tokyo on subway. "Everything was going fine, but somehow the three of us became separated. Walter had no idea where he was and how to make it back to the base. He suddenly found himself alone, amongst millions of people who only two months earlier were ready to defend their country to the death. Walter recognized that as American he was an easy target for anybody looking for revenge. He tried to read the subway schedule but couldn't translate a word. He got on the subway but found himself more lost than before. "Finally, a nice Japanese man recognized that I was lost and helped me find my way back home. I am grateful to that man to this day." In January of 1946 Walter learned there was a ship going back to the United States in ten days and was ordered to be on it. He was going home.

Homecoming

Walter sailed home on the Aircraft Carrier USS Intrepid, now anchored as a museum in the Hudson River in New York City. On the trip back home, he thought hard about his future. The Army had offered him a promotion to Second Lieutenant as an Artillery Officer in Fort Sill, Oklahoma. Walter loved the Army, and the thought of a career was tempting; but he had other things on his mind. He had made a promise he knew he couldn't keep. Walter received letters from Mary Kleinman, the Viennese girlfriend from New York City, Tea Jaegerman his former girlfriend in Hamburg, Georgia Koonce from Phoenix, and Louise Levite his sister Lore's best friend.

USS Intrepid

"Louise always wrote the best letters," Walter remembered. "During the war, the soldiers lived from mail call to mail call. It was our sole connection to home. We would read each letter until the paper eventually fell apart." It was Louise's letters that Walter enjoyed the most.

At first Louise wasn't that impressed with Walter. At the beginning of the war she accompanied Walter's sister Lore on a visit to Ft Dix, in New Jersey, and liked him well enough, but at the time she had several suitors. Louise kept pictures of all of the boys she was interested in taped to a vanity mirror in her bedroom. The young man she liked the best at the time was proudly displayed at the top of the mirror, the rest were positioned below in order of her ranking. In late 1942, Walter's photo was taped to the bottom of Louise's mirror. As the war went on and the two corresponded, Walter's picture gradually ascended up the mirror and by V-J Day, Walter had made it to the top spot. Walter was the one for her.

Walter had promised Georgia Koontz that he would return to her in Phoenix as soon as the war was over and had said nothing to make her think otherwise. She was waiting patiently for him in Arizona. He had also made a promise to his mother that he would return home to her in New York. He knew he would be breaking Georgia's heart, but he decided to go back to New York City. As much as he felt duty bound not to disappoint his mother, what pulled his heart back to New York were Louise's letters. Even though they had yet to go on their first date, Walter felt that Louise was the one for him.

Louise and Walter started seeing each other as soon as he arrived back in town. Walter knew that he needed to have a good job if wanted to impress his new girlfriend. French Fabrics offered Walter his old job back, but he couldn't stand the thought of living in New York As soon as he got home, he remembered why he hated New York City. It was a big, noisy, and unfriendly place. He was glad to see his parents but being in New York made him feel like an immigrant. He wasn't an immigrant. Not anymore.

Like many combat veterans, Walter had a difficult time adjusting to civilian life. "It was hard for me to listen to people tell how much they had suffered during the war. They talked about food and gas rationing and waiting in line for this and that. Then they would talk about how much money they made because of all of the good jobs that were available because the boys were overseas fighting. I'm sure they felt like they suffered, but they never had to spend a night in a foxhole. They never saw their buddies die at their sides."

After avoiding the Holocaust in Europe, Walter lived through his own holocaust during his invasions of Guam, Leyte, and Okinawa. The term PTSD (Post traumatic stress syndrome) was not in use. Rather, terms like shell shock and battle fatigue were often used to describe what the soldiers were going through. Walter was no exception as he suffered from sleepless nights and had trouble adjusting to the noise and bustle of New York City. It wasn't exactly the homecoming experience he was looking for.

At this time more information became public about the horrors of the concentration camps. Learning that all of his family members who were left behind in Germany had been murdered in those camps negated any jubilation about winning the war. Walter needed time to work things out in his mind before he could go on with his life.

He had spent the past few years island hopping across the Pacific, sleeping in tents, foxholes and under the open sky on behalf of his new country. He'd been shot at, bombed, and almost blown up. He was no longer an immigrant when he went to boot camp and became a G. I. He was an American citizen and had put his life on the line to prove it. So when an Army buddy named Wormser, also from Germany, invited him to

Massachusetts to work at his family's leather company, Walter jumped at the chance.

His relationship with Louise was going to have to be long distance. He went to work for the Peabody Leather Finishing Company, found an apartment in Salem, and enrolled in business classes at a college in Boston. For the first time since the Japanese surrender, Walter started to let go of the war and focus on the future. Eventually he had enough money to buy a second-hand 1936 Chevrolet 2-door so he could drive back to see Louise every other weekend.

Walter and his 1936 Chevrolet

"The funny thing about the Peabody Leather Finishing Company is that they didn't have any leather at the time I started working for them," Walter explained. "Because all leather went to support the war effort, there wasn't enough left over to support the fashion industry. To stay in business, the company used artificial leather, which was called vinyl saturated paper. (Today it is called faux leather or pleather.) They stamped the new material in leather patterns and made it into purses, wallets, and belts."

Walter was an immediate success, but after a few months the leather shortage had ended, and the company no longer wanted to work with artificial leather. It was at this time the company asked Walter if he would like to buy their vinyl saturated paper operation for ten thousand dollars.

"I had saved five thousand during the war and managed to get a loan for another five thousand. Before I knew it, I was in the fake leather business."

The Sommers Plastic Company

In 1946 Walter started The Sommers Plastic Company. Much to his chagrin, he realized that to be successful, his company needed to be located in New York City near the Garment District. So within a year of leaving the city, Walter headed back to start his new business. However, the fact that Louise Levite was waiting for him made it easier to return to the city. Now making a good living, Walter decided he could afford to support a wife. He asked Louise Levite to marry him. She didn't hesitate. The answer was yes.

Walter's old boss Mr. Kates at French Fabrics was pleased to have him back in New York and offered him more than enough space in the basement of the building at 135 Madison Avenue at no cost. Using his contacts in Massachusetts and New Hampshire, Walter had material made to sell to various clothing manufacturers in Manhattan and Brooklyn. It didn't take long for Sommers Plastics to take off and Walter realized he needed some help. He hired Herman Schecter to assist him with shipping, receiving, billing, and bookkeeping. "Herman was a real go-getter and had ambition to better himself," Walter remembered. With Herman's help the business began to grow.

Now that Walter felt his future was secure, he and Louise became engaged on Thanksgiving 1947 and married on March 30, 1948.

Louise Levite

LOUISE WAS BORN LIESL-LOTTE-LEVITE IN Straubing, Germany on April 24,1925 to Max Levite and Irma Schwarzhaupt Levite. Straubing is a picturesque Medieval village in Bavaria on the Danube River. The Levites came from Munich, and the Schwarzhaupts had Bavarian roots that traced back to the 16th century. Liesl had a wonderful childhood for her first seven years until 1932, when her mother died tragically of a carbon monoxide leak while taking a bath. It was also at that time that the Nazis came to power and to quote Louise, "terrible things happened.

Excerpt from Louise's diary entry written at age sixteen:

"The day after my 7ᵗʰ birthday my mother suddenly died. Since then things have never been the same. It seems that with my mother's death a chain of misfortunes started. Hitler came to power and my uncle was beaten up, put into prison by the Nazis, and later fled to France. My best friend Gretl's father was murdered by the Nazis. Jewish stores were boycotted, and my father's store was one of them. Terrible things happened in Germany."

Louise in Bavaria

Louise's uncle Fritz was beaten by the Nazis and suffered throughout his life from the trauma of his injuries. Her best friend Gretl's father, Otto Seltz, was taken into a Bavarian forest and murdered by the Nazis. It was later learned that they had misidentified Otto and murdered the wrong person. Louise's family department store, Schwarzhaupts, was boycotted by Nazi decree. Signs were plastered "Don't Buy from the Jews" and Stars of David were painted on store windows.

The "terrible things," Louise called the 1930s continued to grow worse under Nazi rule. With the passing of the Nuremberg laws in 1935, Jews were stripped of their basic rights and privileges, including their citizenship. Louise and her sister Elsie could no longer attend public school. Her father could no longer own property and was forced to sell the family store and the family home for a fraction of their value just as the Sommer family had done in Frankfurt.

In 1937, Max decided it was no longer safe to stay in Germany. He sent Louise and Elsie to visit relatives in England under the pretense that they would return after a short visit. At age 12, Louise and Elsie boarded an eastbound train in the middle of the night, knowing they would never see their home again. They traveled alone, without their father, so it wouldn't call attention to their leaving. They were told not to say goodbye to their friends and not to get emotional when leaving their father at the train station and to act as if they would soon be returning, even though they knew they would not see him for another six months. But the hardest part of that night was saying goodbye to their grandparents, Emma and Karl.

Years later Elsie wrote this about the night they left Germany:

"It would be the last time we would see our beloved grandparents, but no one was to know it was the last time. There were to be no special hugs, no demonstration of love. No one was to know that we would leave Germany in the dark of the night on a train with Nazis checking passports and belongings. The unspoken, the repressed childhood longing for the extra hugs, the reaching for those solid, wonderful people, Emma, and Karl, who remained behind to die in Theresienstadt haunts us. We saw in their eyes that they knew they would never see us again."

Theresienstadt was both a concentration camp and ghetto in Nazi occupied Czechoslovakia. It served two purposes: it was simultaneously a way-station to the death camps in Poland and a "retirement settlement" for elderly and prominent Jews to mislead their communities about the Final Solution. Its conditions were deliberately engineered to hasten the death of its prisoners, and the ghetto also served a propaganda role. Unlike other ghettos, the exploitation of slave labor was not economically important. Theresienstadt, in essence was intended as performance propaganda to mislead the rest of the world about the Holocaust.

"That night at the Straubing train station haunted my mother throughout her life," Louise's daughter, Nancy, explained. "On the few times I heard my mother speak about her escape from Germany, she always had a haunted look, as if something froze inside her that night, as if she were still that 12-year-old child longing to hug her grandparents who she would never see again."

After leaving Germany, Louise and Elsie lived with relatives in London for six months, a time they both described as unbearably lonely and sad, without their father and friends, unable to attend school, uncertain about their future, and haunted by leaving their grandparents in Germany. Six months later, their father Max joined them in London. Instead of returning to Germany, they were on their way to America to live with Max's older brother, Salomon, 'Salo' Levite.

In 1925, Salo Levite had been sent to America, at 17 years of age, to seek his fortune. His conservative Jewish parents viewed him as too ambitious, too worldly, a bad influence on his seven younger siblings. Salo prospered in America, and during the 1930s he became part owner of the Meis Department Store in Danville Illinois. A second store was added when the Meis family bought the Terre Haute Dry Goods Company at 625 Wabash Avenue. Salo moved to Terre Haute, Indiana, but made yearly trips to his family in Bavaria. After Hitler and the Nazis came to power it became evident to Max Levite that Germany was no longer safe for Jews. The Nazis were careful not to let Jewish families send their money out of the country, but as an American citizen, Salo Levite was not under their jurisdiction. During each trip to Germany, Salo carried money to America for his younger brother and eventually Max had enough money to live on when it came time for the family's escape. The brother who had been banished to America as a bad apple was now the family's savior.

Upon arriving in America, Louise recorded her excitement at seeing the Statue of Liberty and the skyscrapers of New York: "I think the Statue of Liberty was waving to me saying "Welcome, Stranger."

It took many years before Louise stopped feeling like a stranger or a refugee in America or stopped feeling marked by her heavy German accent. Her first residence in America was in Terre Haute, where her Uncle Salo lived. Upon arrival in Terre Haute, Salo declared that Liesl-Lotte and Elsa were to lose their German names and assume American names: Liesl-Lotte was assigned the name Louise and Elsa became Elsie. To encourage them to learn English quickly, Salo fined them a penny for every German word spoken. So, after losing their mother, their country, language, and names, Louise and Elsie began the process of becoming Americans, in Terre Haute, Indiana.

Max Levite went into business for himself by buying old car tires and turning them into welcome mats. He sold them door to door and was somewhat successful until World War II started in Europe. Even though America wasn't yet in the war, all salvage rubber was now needed by the manufactures for the war effort and Max's business prospects in rubber were no longer viable.

After living two years in Terre Haute, Max moved with his daughters to New York City, where he went into the glove business manufacturing elegant women's gloves. As it turned out, Julius and Helen Sommer were working at the glove factory—Sonn Gloves—Julius cutting leather and Helen stitching gloves—and Max and Julius became friends. When Julius received his hidden money from the Swiss bank, he was able to invest in the glove business and became Max's business partner. This auspicious business partnership led to another lasting partnership, Louise, and Walter's marriage.

Wedding Day

"It was a cold, snowy day, and it happened at a very nice synagogue on West End Avenue in New York City," Walter said about his wedding day. "Louise's father invited just about everybody he knew. And after the wedding, we were busy shaking hands for over an hour. This much I remember."

Louise before the wedding

At the wedding, Walter met Louise's Uncle Salo. Salo was then president and half owner of the Meis Department Stores in Terre Haute, Indiana. Salo liked what he saw in the twenty-seven-year-old Walter, who had created a profitable business in less than two years after leaving the Army.

"Louise's Uncle Salo asked me if I liked New York City. When I told him that I didn't, he informed me that he was starting a new women's sportswear department at the Meis Store in Terre Haute and asked me if

I would be interested in heading it. I told him that I hated New York but explained that I didn't know a thing about woman's clothes. He told me it didn't matter. He saw what I could do with artificial leather and thought that I could learn what I needed to know once I got to Terre Haute."

Salo Levite

Walter recalled the day the Army transport train had broken down in Terre Haute and the kindness shown to him while standing guard in the snow. It wasn't much to go on when making such an important decision, but Terre Haute and the kind people had made a positive impression on him. Based on that experience alone, Walter accepted the position with Meis Department Store.

In July of 1948 Walter sold Sommers Plastics to Herman Schecter. "At the time Herman didn't have the money, so we worked a deal so he could buy the company for what we had in inventory. Herman was a good man, and I knew he would be successful," Walter said. Throughout the 50s, Sommers Plastics began to introduce and trademark new products, imitation leather like Roller Patent and Marshmallow. The Sommers Plastic Company is still thriving today in Clifton, New Jersey with Schecter's sons, Fred, and Ed at the helm.

Walter Moves to Terre Haute

LABOR DAY 1948—TEMPERATURE WAS 98 degrees—and Walter arrived in Terre Haute on the Spirit of St Louis, ready to begin his new career at Meis. Salo Levite was waiting for him at the train station. Instead of taking him to see the department store on Wabash Avenue he took Walter to the Jewish-only Phoenix Country Club for a round of golf. "It was a nice golf course on the east end of Terre Haute where the members of the small Jewish community could join," Walter explained. "I soon found out that there were prejudices in Indiana just as there had been in Germany.

Salo informed Walter that Jews weren't allowed at most of the clubs around Terre Haute, "so we built this beautiful clubhouse and a golf course of our own." This type of segregation wasn't anything new to Walter, after all, he had been singled out his entire life. He had been called "a less than human Jew" back in Germany. He was a job-stealing immigrant when he arrived in New York City, and a Nazi Kraut when he tried to enlist in the Army. Even after putting his life on the line for his country he wasn't allowed to join the Elks Club in Terre Haute in 1948.

"Some of this was our own fault," Walter explained. "In 1905 the Jewish members in Terre Haute built the old Phoenix Club House on 201 S. 5th Street. The club, which was used for social events and dinners, also had a club room where the men played cards. Shortly after it was built some of the local Christian men wanted to join, but the powers that be at the time said, no. Only Jews could join. Some were offended and in retaliation, wouldn't allow Jews to join their clubs. Today that sounds silly, but those were different times."

Original Phoenix Club

When Walter started at Meis the next day, he realized how much he didn't know about women's sportswear. He was given a tour of the store, then given a budget on how much to spend. In a few days he was headed back to New York on the train, ready to make his first purchases. Walter needed to get up to speed quickly because he was in charge of women's sportswear business.

One of Walter's first purchases in New York didn't go as planned. Salo told Walter to study what was selling well at Bloomingdales in New York. It only made sense that if an item was selling at Bloomindales it ought to sell in Terre Haute. Walter saw a versatile blouse that could be worn 13 different ways. "It was flying off the shelves at Bloomingdales and I was sure it would it was going to be a hit back in Terre Haute. I was so sure I bought 120 blouses and expected it to sell out in days. Bloomingdales had taken a full-page ad out in all of the New York newspapers, so I talked Salo into doing the same with the Terre Haute Star Tribune. We used the same ad add just changed Bloomingdales to Meis. We placed the add to run the day before Thanksgiving, which was one of the busiest shopping days of the year. When the weekend was over, we had sold exactly 7 blouses. I realized that I had a lot to learn about sportswear.

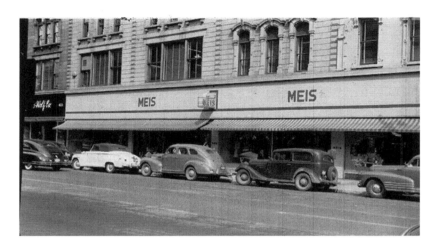

Meis Store on Wabash Avenue in Terre Haute

"Shortly after that I bought some beautiful Angora sweaters that I was confident would be a best seller. One of our best customers bought a sweater for each of her daughters to wear at church on Sunday. I assured her they would be the envy of the congregation. On the very next Monday, the lady stormed into the store demanding a refund because the sweaters had shed over their coats. I tried to explain that it was the nature of Angora to shed, and I couldn't give a full refund for sweaters that had been worn. She exploded and told me that she would never buy another stich of clothing from Meis if I didn't give her a full refund. After buying the blouses that nobody wanted, I was afraid that I had made another bad decision to purchase these Angora sweaters. I apprehensively went to Salo and asked him what to do. Salo told me to give her what she wanted. From that day on, I referred to the woman's daughter as Angora Mary. I had only been there a short time and had bought a 120 blouses that nobody wanted and almost lost one of the store's best customers. I wasn't off to the greatest start."

In November 1948, Louise and the couple's son Ron, joined Walter in Terre Haute. Walter and Louise bought their first home, a tiny bungalow on Monterey Avenue, for $11,000. In 1951, when their daughter Nancy was born, the family needed a larger home, and moved to a spacious ranch house on South 23rd Street, purchased for $22,000. By this time Walter had established himself in the business community and was a successful, well-respected businessman. Louise, who had earned a degree in botany from Hunter College in New York, chose to become a homemaker, raising her children and supporting her husband as he concentrated on his career. Louise was a woman of her times, a devoted wife and mother, who excelled at everything, especially organizing her children's school projects and their birthday parties. Her talents seemed limitless; she knew how to do so many things, easily and confidently. Both Ron and Nancy say that they won the mom lottery.

Louise and Walter were active volunteers in Terre Haute's civic arena. In 1962, Louise's empathy for children led her to establish Terre Haute's Clothes Closet organization to ensure that Vigo County schoolchildren would have sturdy and warm winter coats, boots, and mittens. She led the organization for more than 20 years, directing a committee of women who collected clothes, washed, and mended them when necessary, organized and catalogued them by size and type and distributed them to schoolchildren.

In 1963, an article in the *Terre Haute Tribune* described Louise and her Clothes Closet committee as "fiercely determined that no child attending school in Vigo County would be without adequate clothing."

Louise loved to take bouquets to her friends and neighbors — lilacs from her spring garden, zinnias and Black-eyed Susans from her summer garden. She faithfully brought matzoh ball soup to sick friends, apple strudel to new neighbors, and her signature apple kuchen or bundt kuchen to members of the Temple Israel Congregation whose days needed some sweetness.

Louise was an accomplished cook and liked to organize large dinner parties for friends and family, always designing the serving platters to balance colors and textures. Although most comfortable with her aunt's German recipes, pickling and brining tongue and corned beef, sauerbraten, and sauerkraut, she mastered American cooking as well.

According to her daughter, Nancy, when asked what made her food so wonderful, her mother would smile and say, "All recipes have a secret ingredient — *love*."

Walter, Ron, Nancy and Louise

Louise used her botany education to grow spectacular flowers in her gardens. She found the natural world of gardens and meadows, forests, and mountains, to be sources of beauty and comfort. She could walk into a field of clovers and with a touch of magic reach down to pluck the one four-leaf clover, which she often taped inside birthday cards for family and friends. Each fall she took Ron and Nancy on nature hikes through Indiana parks and identified each tree by their bark and leaves. Ron still jokes that he could name every tree in Deming Park thanks to his mother's tutelage.

Louise loved being the Den Mother for Ron's Cub Scouts. Ron recalls how fortunate the Troop was to have his mom as their leader. One fond memory was the crafting and creation of an after-school art project we did while sitting around the ping pong table in the basement of our South 23rd Street family home. "We chose from an assortment of dry lentils, corn, a variety of beans, peas, and pastas as our color palate. Then we affixed and arranged the dry food on carboard using Elmer's glue. With my mom's encouragement and guidance, we had fun, made art, and learned how to appreciate and value the bounty of nature."

Nancy recalls asking her mother for help baking an apple pie for a 4-H project. "Every girl there will be making apple pies," Louise told her.

"The judges will be sick of apple pies. You need to make a Bundt Kuchen." Nancy objected, but Louise convinced her to bake the Kuchen. Nancy entered the bundt kuchen in the Vigo County Fair and won the blue ribbon.

While Louise concerned herself with the children, Walter concentrated on his career. That meant the work didn't end just because the store closed. Walter often brought work home with him. After work he would tally sales tickets and tags to see if he met the day's sales quota. Both Ron and Nancy helped Walter as he went through the tickets and sorted them.

"The colors—those are what I remember most vividly about the nightly ritual of the ticket game," Nancy recalled in an essay she published about her father, "The Language of Coats":

Sometime in the early evening, while my mother cleaned up the kitchen and my brother counted his baseball cards, my father and I would sit at our dining room table, sorting and organizing tickets from the coats he had sold that day. Tickets were laid out by size— green upon green, orange upon orange—then by manufacturer's style number, and then by price. As manager of the coat department in my uncle's department store, my father needed to know which styles and sizes had sold that day in order to know which coats to reorder and which to ship back to the manufacturer.

While my brother took great pride in knowing, to the decimal point, the batting averages of Mickey Mantle and Roger Maris, I prided myself upon recognizing the range of colors and sizes of the tickets—the tangerine-colored size 16, the pale green size 18, or the violet size 24' reciting with my father the vocabulary of coats: cashmeres, camel hairs, tweeds, with rabbit, squirrel, raccoon, or muskrat collars, sewn-on or detached.

Aside from these tickets, my father didn't have much emotional or financial security. An immigrant from Europe, he had lost contact with his language and culture, and found himself in Terre Haute, Indiana, a town where people lived generation after generation, growing up in the houses their great-great-grandparents had built. We had our modest ranch house at 134 South 23rd Street, but no ancestral home, no family reunions, no burial plots. People in Terre Haute thought my father exotic; they couldn't place his dark, Semitic looks, often asking him where he came from, or if he was related to Ricky Ricardo.

Even though he had just survived Hitler, my father said that nothing had ever happened to him, he said he was a simple person. "I'm nobody famous," he would say. His experience in 1930s Germany taught him to stay inconspicuous, avoid controversy, never wear, or say anything out of the ordinary. Such a modest profile was perfectly suited for the department store business, a business in which it was best if a manager was never observed driving too fast or speaking too loudly, such actions reflecting poorly upon the character of the store.

The customer is always right, my father would tell us—even if the customer tried on every size 18 available but bought nothing or asked to open the store early or stay late while she decided between the full-length- fur-lined tweed coat and the three-quarter length fur-collared and cuffed camel hair. On a good day, in season, my father might sell forty coats: the day after Christmas, three hundred. But then there were the days when the sales clerks quarreled or were sick, the competition undersold him, or customers wanted herringbone-tweed and he had only plaid. Those were the days in which he didn't make his day. "Making your day" was department store language for selling the amount of merchandise you predicted you could sell, based on previous years' sales. Despite rain, sleet, hail, markdowns and willful customers, a manager was expected to make or exceed his day, every day, day after day. Meager raises or Christmas bonuses, money my father needed to establish some roots in Terre Haute, depended on him making his day.

Because Walter arrived in America at age 18 with only a single quarter in his pocket, he felt the need to work as hard as he could to provide the security for his family that he himself had lost. Until 1933 Walter was raised by a wealthy family who could trace its roots back for hundreds of years. His family thrived during the depression and his father's business expanded. But then Hitler and the Nazis took everything from them. Life had taught him that his security could be taken away without any warning by circumstances beyond his control. He was determined that his children would never experience what he did as a teenager. "Those were bad times in Germany," Walter recounted. "I tried to keep that part of my life behind me. I tried to plan for every contingency. I wanted to make sure there was money for our children's education along with our retirement. Louise and I may have not been the best parents in the world, but we prepared them to have success in life. And I couldn't be prouder of how they turned out."

Like Walter, Louise was also haunted by her memories of Nazi Germany. She made sure to insulate her children from the cruel fate their family had suffered during the holocaust. Looking back only brought pain, so nothing was ever spoken about the Nazi era. But her experiences growing up in Nazi Germany, and her arrival in America as a refugee, left her with a deep well of empathy and a strong sense of duty to welcome and care for new neighbors and refugees, as if their safety and happiness were central to her own.

Louise loved being a mom. She wanted to raise children with American names — names an ocean away from her German name, Liesl-Lotte. She loved her children's names — Ron and Nancy — and she loved their American childhood, saving all their elementary school workbooks, papers, projects, ribbons, corsages, and baseball cards. To make sure they identified as American, Walter and Louise refused to speak German at home.

According to Walter, Ron was the All-American boy. He loved baseball, collected baseball cards, and memorized all the statistics on the back of the card. He was active in Boy Scouts and never got in any trouble. He got good grades and did whatever was asked of him.

Nancy, on the other hand, seemed to march to a different drummer. Walter likes to tell the story of how Nancy and her friends spent one Halloween evening throwing rotten tomatoes at the front porches around their neighborhood. "She spent the following night cleaning the front porches under the supervision of the Terre Haute Police Department," Walter laughed. "To say she was strong willed is a bit of an understatement." He also boasts about the time when after graduating from Northwestern University, Nancy refused a car ride home and made the 200-mile trek from Chicago to Terre Haute on her bicycle instead. Walter also likes to point out that after all of Nancy's education, she got a job at a chicken farm. "I told her I was happy that she was gainfully employed, but maybe she might try to find a better job than giving shots to chickens," Walter joked. In reality he was proud of Nancy. She had volunteered at a kibbutz in Israel and didn't want to be stuck in the kitchen or doing laundry like the other girls. She declared that she wanted an adventure and argued that she was capable of doing the same work as the young men, so they assigned her to one of the dirtiest jobs. Her assignment was to feed, inoculate, and clean-up after the kibbutz's substantial flock of chickens. Walter always finishes the story that it wasn't long before she got a job teaching at the Jerusalem University.

Despite being immersed in their American lives, Walter and Louise were still influenced by their time under Nazi rule. Nancy recalls having three heavy-duty locks on their front door. "That should keep the Nazis out!" Walter would say. Part of him still blamed his mother for letting the Nazis into their home to take his father to Buchenwald. In reality, there was nothing his mother could have done, but it was the perception that the locks stood as a barrier between the family and the evil that loomed outside the door.

Louise would never throw away leftover food. Whatever couldn't be eaten within a day or two, would be dated and placed into the freezer. Additionally, food was bought for the freezer—and stayed in the freezer for decades. According to Nancy the food would be meticulously dated, wrapped, and arranged for future use but never used. When Nancy suggested to her parents that frozen food actually didn't improve with age, they shrugged and replied, "It doesn't get any worse either." Louise didn't believe in expiration dates when it came to frozen food. She believed that food stayed safer in the freezer. Walter agreed with Louise on the subject. "Frozen food isn't old; it has historical significance."

Growing up in 1930s Germany, Walter and Louise learned that life can swiftly divide into before and after. After settling in Terre Haute, Indiana, in 1948, they were determined to put the past behind them. They wanted to lose their accents and settle into a middle-class American life. As much as they tried, the lessons learned in Nazi Germany still had an effect on their day-to-day life. There was a fear that everything could be taken away at the drop of a hat. After moving to Indiana, Walter and Louise wouldn't travel without their passports as proof of their American citizenship in case the family needed to flee across state and national borders. Louise hid Swiss francs in her lingerie drawer in case of emergency. Despite living in the security of mid-century America, they were still haunted by the past. Walter and Louise did everything in their power to blend in as the traditional American Family and not to stand out as German-Jewish immigrants. They wanted to make sure that Ron and Nancy never experienced the extreme prejudice they endured before coming to the United States.

Walter Makes a Stand Against Segregation

EVEN THOUGH WALTER NO LONGER felt the sting of anti-Semitism in Terre Haute, he was aware of the plight of Black America in his adopted hometown. In the early 1960's, the Meis Department Store was the major anchor store on Wabash Avenue and Walter had achieved a measure of status in the local business community. He had been promoted from women's sportswear to women's coats. The women's coat department at Meis was the most important and the most profitable in the entire store. After a busy morning at the store, Walter decided to reward some employees by taking them to lunch at the upscale Terre Haute House.

After finding an open table, they were reviewing their menu when a waitress approached and informed Walter that she couldn't serve them because of the manner in which they were seated. "What's wrong with the way we are sitting?" Walter asked.

"I can't serve him," the waitress said and nodded at the man sitting next to Walter.

At first Walter didn't understand what she meant until he realized that the employee sitting next to him was African American. Walter felt a righteous anger rise up inside of him. He remembered the time in North Carolina when in order to make room for him a black family was forced to get off of the bus. He remembered the segregated rest rooms and water fountains in the south—and he remembered his own persecution in Germany under the Nazis. He remembered what it felt like when he saw the sign in the Frankfurt City Park that stated that neither dogs nor Jews were allowed to sit on the benches. He remembered how it felt when he was told that he was subhuman. He had gone to war and put his life on the line to free people who lived thousands of miles away. He was not going to tolerate this type of behavior in Terre Haute, Indiana.

"You will serve us exactly as we are seated or I will never eat here again," Walter declared with resolve. "More than that, I will make sure that nobody from Meis will eat here either."

The waitress was stunned and didn't know how to reply. After an uncomfortably long period of time, she turned and went to consult the restaurant manager. Walter wasn't sure if he had overplayed his hand. He was counting on the manager not wanting to offend a department head from the Meis Store, given that their employees represented a substantial part of the restaurant's business.

Fortunately, the gamble paid off and the waitress reappeared at the table. "What would you gentlemen like to eat?" she asked as though nothing out of the ordinary had happened.

That was the beginning of the end of segregation in Terre Haute restaurants. Over the next few days, Walter repeated the act in other restaurants and within weeks black patrons were welcome in all downtown restaurants. All it took was one determined man to say stand up and say, "No! This is wrong and I'm not going to tolerate it!"

"At the time, black people could only eat at the lunch counters in the dime stores," Walter explained. "They weren't allowed to eat at the nicer restaurants in town. It was a bad practice, and I am proud to have played a small role in changing things."

As the years passed, Walter continued producing the sales needed to keep Salo Levite happy. "Salo was a harsh taskmaster," Walter explained. "He expected sales' goals to be met on a daily basis. He worked hard and expected his employees to do the same. He was a retail genius."

Walter recalled April 16, 1951. the night Louise gave birth to Nancy. "The store stayed open late on Monday and Thursday nights. "As luck would have it, Louise went into Labor on a Monday evening," Walter remembered. "Why can't she have the baby on a night when we close early?" Salo complained. "I reminded him that Louise was his favorite niece and he begrudgingly told me to go take care of my wife. It's a good thing I went when I did. Nancy was born less than one hour after I received the call." Walter admits that Salo was joking, but the story shows the pressure Walter was under to reach his sales goals.

Walter's long hours and retail success paid off for himself and for the Meis Store. He met his sales' goals and was promoted to vice-president. And Meis expanded, opening up ten more department stores across the Midwest. As the years went by, Walter no longer spent nights counting the coats sold at the Wabash Avenue store. Instead of riding the train to New York, he flew from store to store on the corporate jet, overseeing the operations of all the stores in the chain. Ron had become a successful attorney and Nancy was establishing herself as a college professor and writer. Louise kept busy with her gardening and philanthropic pursuits. Walter enjoyed the fast-pace challenges he faced as vice-president, and he planned on working as long as the job was fulfilling. But in 1988 Meis was sold to the Brown Shoe Company. After working for Meis for over 40 years, Walter had a decision to make.

"I thought about working for Brown, but they were nothing but a bunch of bean counters," Walter explained. "They didn't care about setting fashion trends or buying clothes that would set our stores apart from the others. All they were concerned with was the profit margin on every item. Style and quality didn't matter. Under those conditions Walter decided to retire. "I had an extremely good run at Meis for forty years, and I decided to end my career on a positive note."

Retirement

After two months of retirement, Walter needed to find something to keep himself busy. Walter is proud that he was the first Jewish member of the Masonic Lodge in Terre Haute. Part of the Masonic mission statement encourages its members to get involved in local charities. Walter was grateful for everything America had done for him and decided that it would only be appropriate to give something back. "I come from a volunteering family. I don't know any different. Giving to others, helping others — to me, that was important."

Walter first volunteered for three organizations—Red Cross, Hospice, and Union Hospital of Terre Haute— to help people who couldn't help themselves. He felt that by helping people who were suffering, he would be honoring his aunts and uncles who had died in the Holocaust.

A few years later, a member of the Terre Haute Library recruited Walter to teach English as a second language to foreign students at Indiana State University. As a young boy Walter realized the importance of learning multiple languages. He had learned English, French, and Spanish in his German primary school and felt that this helped him become successful in America. "Learning different languages opened the entire world for me," Walter explained. "My father struggled in America because he didn't speak any English. My mother spoke a little French and English, so she had an easier time adjusting as we started our new life in New York. It only seemed natural to help foreign students at Indiana State learn English. Walter quickly became popular with his students and decided to broaden their cultural horizon by taking them to CANDLES Holocaust Museum. "I was surprised to learn that they knew nothing about how the Jews were treated in Germany under the Nazis."

In 1993 Walter took a Korean student, Myousun Kim, to the museum and not only introduced her to the story of the Holocaust but also explained the historical causes of why it happened in a way that she could easily understand. CANDLES founder Eva Moses Kor was at the museum that day and eavesdropped on their conversation. She was taken aback by Walter's thoughtful explanations and historical analysis, as well as the way that Myousun responded to Walter's presentation. Never one to mince words, Eva pulled Walter aside and forcefully asked him to resign from the library and become a docent at CANDLES. At this time, Eva and Walter were casual acquaintances and she had never heard his personal story. But she saw enough in his patient interaction with Myousun to realize that Walter's grasp of European history and his personal perspective of the Holocaust needed to be heard. "You need to be here." Eva told him. "People need to hear your story."

Myousun Kim and Walter have remained lifelong friends. She operates a large English School in Seoul South Korea. Walter likes to joke; "If you ever hear a Korean speaking English with a German accent, you can assume they went to Myousun's school."

Walter was flattered and thanked Eva but explained that he needed to talk it over with Louise. That evening Walter told Louise about Eva's offer. Louise pondered in silence for a moment and quietly said: "You have an obligation, so people won't forget."

On the very next day, Walter accepted the position and became a docent and lecturer at CANDLES. He didn't know it at the time, but at seventy years of age, he was about to embark on a journey that would forever change his life and touch the lives of people in the Wabash Valley.

Eva Kor and Walter at Candles

Eva Kor

EVA MOSES KOR (JANUARY 31, 1934-July 4, 2019) It would be hard to find anyone in the Wabash Valley who hasn't heard of Eva Kor. The diminutive Romanian-born Holocaust survivor, who suffered from the horrors of Auschwitz as a child, became a beacon of hope for the entire world.

Eva and her twin sister Miriam were subjected to human experimentation at the hands of SS Doctor Joseph Mengele at the Auschwitz Concentration camp in German occupied Poland. Eva's parents and two older sisters were killed in the gas chambers of Birkenau upon arrival at the camp. Eva and Miriam were spared because Mengele, known as The Angel of Death, wanted twins to use in his experiments.

The entire Moses family was deported from the Cehei Ghetto in May of 1944 to Auschwitz-Birkenau. After a four-day journey in a cattle car, the family was forced into a line with other new arrivals. The purpose of the line was to decide who would be used as a worker and who was to go directly to the gas chambers. While in line, a SS office approached Eva's mother and demanded to know if Eva and Miriam were twins. When she answered yes, the girls were taken away despite their mother's protests. Her mother and sisters crying along the railroad tracks with outstretched arms was the last image Eva would have of her family as they were whisked away to the gas chamber.

Eva and Miriam were subjected to deplorable experiments by Dr. Mengele. Eva later recounted Mengele's daily regimen at the camp. On Mondays, Wednesdays, and Fridays, the Nazi doctors would put Eva and Miriam, along with numerous other twins, naked in a room for six to eight hours and then measure every part of their bodies. On Tuesdays,

Thursdays, and Saturdays, SS doctors would take the twins to a blood lab and tie their arms to restrict blood flow. Several samples of blood would be taken from the left arm while a minimum of five injections with unknown substances would be given in the right arm.

On January 27, 1945, the Soviet Red Army liberated Auschwitz. Eva and Miriam were among the 180 children who survived the camp.

1Eva Moses Kor and her sister Miriam at the liberation of Auschwitz

In 1978, after NBC's miniseries *The Holocaust* aired, Eva and Miriam, began locating other survivors of the experiments. It was from this beginning that Eva conceived the idea of a Holocaust museum in Terre Haute. Eva founded the organization CANDLES, an acronym for "Children of Auschwitz Nazi Deadly Lab Experiments Survivors." Through this program she located 122 other survivors of Mengele.

In 1984, Kor founded the CANDLES Holocaust and Education Center in Terre Haute to educate the public about eugenics, the Holocaust, and the power of forgiveness. Walter recalled meeting Eva Kor when she first arrived in Terre Haute. "The Jewish Community in Terre Haute was very small so we all knew of each other. We had used Eva as a realtor and were what I would call casual acquaintances at the time. She seemed to be distant and unhappy. That was until she made a trip back to Auschwitz and was able to come to grips and eventually forgive the Nazis. It was amazing;

she returned a different person, and the rest is history. Out of the darkness of Auschwitz, Eva Kor became a shining light for the entire world."

Much like Eva, a trip back to Germany allowed Walter to come to terms with what had happened to his family under the Nazis. In 1992 Walter and Louise took part in The Visiting Program of the City of Frankfurt, which invited Jewish residents who were forced to flee Germany due to Nazi persecution, to return to their homeland for reconciliation and in many cases closure.

For many years Walter had avoided reading about the horrors of the Holocaust or thinking about the devastation it had done to his family. All of his aunts and uncles along with cousins and countless friends perished in the concentration camps. But everything changed in 1992 when Walter returned to his hometown. It was on the 1992 trip to Frankfurt that Walter and Louise met Angelika Rieber, a guide and liaison for the Frankfurt Visiting Program. Angelika took Walter to his boyhood home, his old school, and the building that had served as headquarters for Wittwe Hassan, the chain of stores owned by his father. Angelika also scheduled meetings with people that shared similar stories of the Holocaust. This allowed Walter to deal not only with the facts, but also with his feelings that had been suppressed for fifty years. Walter realized that he had a story to tell, a story unique to him, yet with a common thread t0 millions of Jews who suffered under the Nazis.

Angelika Rieber became a lifelong friend of Walter and Louise and has written a book detailing the history of the Sommer Family through several generations.

Walter used a "look forward, never back" policy for his entire life. It had served him well in America. He had excelled in the Army and was a success in the business world. He had planned for his children's education along with his retirement. He always felt that there wasn't any point of looking back to the heartache of the Holocaust. He couldn't change the past. He could only plan for the future, for what was ahead of him, and hope for the best.

A case in point would be made by Ron Sommers in a speech at the Frankfurt Visitors program for the Children of Survivors. "When they came to the United States, my parents literally turned their backs on Germany. I was raised in the Midwest of the United States. Although my parents, my grandparents, and my ancestors came from Germany, there was really no German spoken in our house. There might have been a silent German word, but there was no spoken German during my youth. I am an assimilated German Jew. That's who I am. I don't speak German and I did not learn German."

Walter indeed had turned his back on Germany. He had become an American success story and had buried his 19 years in Germany in the emotional past.

However, his acceptance of Eva Kor's position as a CANDLES docent and the trip to Germany changed everything. What he saw on that trip gave him a new mission for his life. When Walter decided to lecture about the Holocaust, he only knew one way to go about it. If he was going to teach people about what happened in Germany, he was going to be the best prepared teacher he could be. Walter studied everything he could read about the Holocaust, including the most distinguished works of 20th century European history. He became a holocaust scholar. Not only did he teach the horrible facts of the Holocaust, but he also analyzed its cultural and religious causes and its roots in European history. Most importantly, he cautioned how it could all happen again if we fail to learn from our history.

As Walter began to lecture at CANDLES it became abundantly clear that people responded to him in a way that was unique. He is a storyteller by nature and his stories connected with museum visitors in a way that made the bleak events of the past seem real. He especially found common ground with teenagers as he described growing up in Germany under the Nazis. Students became mesmerized by Walters's stories; he made history come alive, vivid, so much more than a footnote in a history book. In Walter they met a witness who barely escaped Germany after Kristallnacht. He experienced the Holocaust as a teenager and therefore had the ability to paint a picture through the eyes of a teenager. In his stories, Walter plays down the hardships he endured in Germany, even though he lost a dozen family members. He points out that his hardships pale in comparison to millions of victims who died in the camps. Yet because of his first-hand experience Walter has legitimate credibility as a Holocaust educator on many different levels. The obvious reason is of course being a Jew who lived in Frankfurt during the rise of the Nazi regime. He also has credibility to speak as a loyal German. Before 1933 he and his family were all proud German Nationalists. His father and uncles all served in the German Army during World War I. He is proud that his maternal Grandfather was awarded the Iron Cross by the King of Prussia, himself.

After leaving Germany, Walter experienced life in New York as an immigrant and a refugee. It gives him credibility to talk about life as a victim of prejudice in America. Walter came under heavy fire as an artilleryman during three major Pacific campaigns. During the war he witnessed death and destruction on a wholesale level. He still has nightmares about killing a Japanese Soldier who was on a suicide run to kill the men in his unit. He witnessed the aftermath of the war in occupied Japan after Hiroshima. He speaks with credibility as a war hero and witness to the horrors of modern warfare.

Walter had a successful business career. He was a devoted father and husband. He was active with his temple and local charities which gives him credibility as a productive member of society. When Walter saw discrimination in Terre Haute in the 1960s, he did something about it. Because of the part he played in desegregating the Terre Haute restaurants, he has credibility as a civil rights activist. After spending his retirement in the service of others, Walter has credibility as a philanthropist. When it came time to serve as a docent and Holocaust educator at CANDLES, Walter studied 20th century European History and made himself a scholar on the subject.

After having his German citizenship revoked as a teenager, Walter was forced to jump through an unlikely set of hoops to obtain citizenship from the United States. For the past 75 years Walter has been a proud American and has a special appreciation for the freedoms most Americans take for granted. Since most of the people to whom Walter speaks are from the

United States, he has the authority to speak to them as a fellow American. On more than one occasion, Germany has offered to restore his German Citizenship. Walter's response is always the same. "Thanks, but no thanks. I am happy to be an American."

No matter who Walter talks to about the Holocaust, he has the credibility necessary to educate and weave a cautionary tale of warning. "If we don't know our history," Walter likes to say, "We will more than likely repeat our mistakes.

"Most of the people who come to CANDLES want to learn about Eva Kor's story and her time at Auschwitz," Walter explained. "She has always been what you might call the museum's star attraction. What I have tried to do is explain what took place that allowed things to get so bad. Most Germans were and are by nature good people and only through a series of improbable events did the Holocaust come about. I've tried to teach about what led up to the Holocaust so people will understand why it happened in hopes that it will never happen again."

Eva Kor was a shining light who came out of the darkness of the Holocaust. Her story of surviving Auschwitz is inspirational. Yet it was Eva's ability to forgive the Nazis in light of the atrocities they committed against her and her family that defies understanding. She found peace by bestowing her forgiveness to those who had wronged her so savagely. Even though she forgave, she wanted to make sure that nobody ever forgets what was done during the Holocaust.

Much like Eva Kor, Walter has also forgiven the Nazis for what they had done. After suppressing memories of his youth, Walter has come to terms with the past. During one of Walter and Louise's trips to Germany, Walter reconnected with a school friend who became a member of the Nazi Party. "Those were bad times in Germany," Walter explained. "And people did what they had to stay alive. It's hard for Americans to understand how Germans are taught to follow orders without question. During this trip, Walter and his friend took a hike in the Tanus Mountains, as they had done so often as school friends. While hiking, the friend had a heart attack and Walter performed CPR to save his life. That physical act of saving a friend's life, a friend who had been a Nazi, touched Walter deeply and allowed him to open up his own heart, to redefine what had happened to him—and to forgive. Hatred did nothing for him; hatred felt like a stone in his own heart. He was able to forgive, but like Eva, he was determined not to let the world forget.

Walter's lectures about the Holocaust include his opinion that if Germany had been treated after World War I in the same manner as after World War II, Adolf Hitler would never have come to power. He blames the Treaty of Versailles for creating the environment that allowed the Nazis to come to power. "France and England wanted to punish Germany for World War I, so the terms of the treaty were so severe, there wasn't any way for Germany to live up to its part of the bargain," Walter explained. "America could have made a difference, but Woodrow Wilson went home before the treaty was signed and France and England did as they pleased. Those conditions and Hitler's hatred for the Jews are the root cause of the Holocaust."

Walter is Awarded the Cross of the Order of Merit

In winter 2016, a group of German citizens visited CANDLES on a day when Walter was scheduled to speak. Once they learned that he was a German Jew, they decided to stay for his lecture. As Walter started to speak one of the Germans called out, "Go ahead and give us hell!" Walter smiled and calmly delivered his lecture in a calm non-accusatory manner. He presented the facts and pointed out that life for Jews in pre-Hitler Germany was no different that living in America today. His family loved Germany and with the exception of the 12 years of Nazi rule, Germany had been good to the Sommer Family. He talked about forgiveness and reconciliation. At the conclusion of the lecture, the group of Germans thanked him for his unbiased approach to the speech. Walter shook hands with everyone and thought nothing further about the encounter.

Walter may have forgotten about that day, but the Germans in attendance had not. They returned to Germany to promote Walter's story of reconciliation, to their families and associates. At the same time, Walter's dear friend Angelika, who had received the Cross of the Order of Merit—Germany's highest civilian award (similar to the American Medal of Freedom)—nominated Walter for the same award.

In the summer of 2016, Walter received a call from the German Consul General in Chicago informing him that German President Joachim Gauck was awarding him the Cross of the Order of Merit of the Federal Republic of Germany. The award was being presented in recognition of his exceptional services in promoting peace and tolerance among peoples and cultures through Holocaust education. Walter responded by saying that they had the wrong Walter Sommers. They assured him that it was not a mistake and that they were planning a public presentation of the award at CANDLES.

At age 95, Walter Sommers a received a standing ovation after receiving the medal and shaking hands with the German Consul General, Herbert Quell. Quell explained why Walter was chosen for the award. "President Gauck has awarded you this high distinction for your outstanding contribution to German-American relations and better understanding. This life of volunteerism and reconciliation with your country of birth formed the basis for being chosen for the award."

Herbert Quell presents Award to Walter

Quell went on to say: "As a docent with the authority of your personal life experience, you have, for the past twenty years or so, engaged yourself in talking about Jewish history in Germany and Europe. You have promoted a realistic, non-defamatory image of my country. You have presented the long-standing commitment of the Federal Republic of Germany to become and to act as a reliable and responsible democracy respecting and implementing human rights."

"Through your voluntary work of roughly two decades, you have reached many people who are interested in Germany. You have invested time and energy in telling people that beyond the twelve years of the Nazi terror regime, there lies a rich history in which Jews played an essential role."

"You have put present-day politics of Germany in context and contributed to the knowledge of my country," Quell said. "It seems that in this process, you also redefined your own relationship with Germany."

Seven decades after fleeing Germany, Walter had been recognized for his good works by the country he loved.

After receiving the Order of Merit award Walter continued to lecture twice a week at CANDLES just as he had done before. However, because of the publicity that came with the award, people began to refer to him as a hero. Walter, who modestly downplays everything when it comes to himself or his accomplishments, dismissed the attention as hyperbole. "I'm just an ordinary guy who just did the best that I could under the conditions that I found myself," Water explained. "Eva Kor was a hero. Her story of survival at Auschwitz was courageous and inspirational. I'm no hero. When I'm gone, I want people to remember me as a family man who lived a wonderful life."

While Walter continued his work at CANDLES, Louise began to show the first signs of dementia. "Part of our autumn ritual was to rake the leaves in our yard. Louise always loved the outdoors and we had gathered leaves together every year of our married life. It never seemed like work. We always enjoyed the time together," Walter remembered. "One day I was working in the front yard, and I realized I hadn't seen Louise in a while. I looked around and couldn't find her anywhere. After a second search, I found her laying down in a pile of leaves. I thought she had suffered a heart attack, but she opened her eyes and said she had simply gotten tired and decided to take a nap in the leaves. I was heartbroken. I knew then that we had to go somewhere where she could receive constant care. That very night our son Ron made arrangements for us to get an assisted living apartment at Westminster Village."

Walter continued to stay busy even after the move to Westminster Village. He still delivered lectures twice a week, but unfortunately, Louise's conditioned worsened, and Walter found himself more isolated. His days at CANDLES became more and more important to him. Walter also continued to receive more recognition as the local NBC affiliate produced a two-part feature on Walter as a Hometown Hero. The story highlighted his life from Kristallnacht to his Army Service in World War II, culminating with his receiving the Order of Merit. Walter liked the attention, but again argued with the notion that he was a hero.

Shortly after Walter's 98th birthday I was approached by Mike Brooks, Pastor of Hope of Israel Church about writing Walter's biography. I met Walter just as he was finishing his lecture to a group of high school students from Indianapolis. He was more than willing to work on this biography but kept repeating, "I don't know why anybody would want to read a book about me." It has been a fascinating two years chronicling why this book had to be written.

In December 2019, friends and family came from as far as Germany to celebrate Walter's 99th birthday. Walter and Louise thoroughly enjoyed being the center of attention. Local television stations and newspapers covered the event and plans were made for an extravaganza celebration for Walters 100th birthday in 2020.

Like the rest of the world the Covid-19 Pandemic brought unforeseen hardships for Walter and Louise. On March 1, 2020, Westminster Village was put on complete quarantine lockdown. Walter desperately missed his weekly CANDLES trips, especially missed the intellectual stimulation and emotional connections he received from talking with museum visitors. Unfortunately, Louise's dementia had progressed to the point that she could no longer have meaningful conversations with Walter. With the pandemic lockdown, Walter's daily, purposeful life was upended: he was not allowed to go to the museum or to Westminster's sport center, which was part of his daily routine to keep physically active; and he could no longer receive weekly visitors who dined with him and savored his stories. Walter and Louise were not allowed to leave the 5th floor and for weeks were not allowed outside their apartment. Isolation began to takes its toll on Walter. "I thought I'd seen everything," Walter lamented. "I guess if you live long enough, you're bound to see something new. The Nazis didn't lock me down like this tight." Eventually, Terry Fear, a close, family friend was allowed to visit Walter and Louise regularly. In the fall of 2020, I was allowed to meet with Walter outside as long as we stayed six feet apart.

Unfortunately, in October 2020, Louise's health further deteriorated, and she peacefully passed away on November 30, 2020, at the age of 95.

Terry Fear performed the burial service for Louise on December 2. On December 13, 2020, the unthinkable happened: Terry Fear unexpectedly passed away. In a period of two weeks, Walter had lost his wife of 73 years along with his best friend. He was devastated. "I had been careful to plan for every contingency in life, but I never planned for this," Walter mourned. "All my life I've looked at the situation and carried on the best I could, That's all I know how to do."

After Terry's passing, Steve was allowed to visit Walter on a daily basis and generously stepped in to fill the void left by Terry's death. Walter and Steve spend their afternoons talking history and politics, comforting each other, and working through their grief, one day at a time. On December 29, 2020, Walter celebrated his 100th birthday. Instead of honoring Walter with the extravagant party that was planned, only Ron, Nancy, Josh, and Steve celebrated the day with him.

On the occasion of Walter's 100th birthday, Ron made a toast to his dad: "Dad your life has been meaningful and purposeful, and you have used your talents to make a difference in your community. As a result of your early life experiences, you chose a pathway to speak your truth about hate and intolerance in a world beset with many challenges. You have given your story to the world, intentionally, sincerely, and passionately, and your work has not been unnoticed. You have inspired others to have the courage to stand up for the fair and equal treatment that all people deserve. You are respected, acknowledged, and loved by your family and your community, and Terre Haute, as your adopted home, is so very fortunate to have you as one of its residents. Your family, friends, and community are grateful that you have been a part of our lives. I love you, dad!"

CANDLES organized a campaign to send 100 birthday cards to Walter on his 100th birthday. The response was overwhelming as 350 cards appeared in his mailbox. Local television stations marked the event along with The Terre Haute Star Tribune. Terre Haute Mayor Duke Bennet proclaimed December 29, 2020, to be Walter Sommers Day. Birthday cards came from all over the world, especially from museum visitors who felt blessed to have met Walter and felt as if they touched history listening to his stories. One person wrote to Walter: "To know you is to know that this is one more day that hate loses. This is one more day young people like me can learn from you and choose to do what is right for our future. In you, our world knows the very best of humanity."

Walter enjoying the Birthday Cards on his 100th Birthday.

Walter has always considered optimism important: "Optimism has kept me going from the very start," he reflected at age 100. "I come from a very optimistic family, and I come from a volunteering family. I don't know any different. Giving to others, helping others — to me, that is important."

In an interview, Tribune-Star columnist Mark Bennett asked Walter for advice about enduring this pervasive pandemic, its disruptions and heartaches. Given Walter's century of experiences, he considered him to be an excellent source. When asked, Walter offered humble, simple, wise suggestions. "Get plenty of sleep, eat well and wear a mask," he said. "Have faith. That's all. We'll get through it."

"Have faith and we'll get through it," has been a creed that Walter has lived by.

The following excerpt is from a letter that Nancy wrote to her father on his 100ᵗʰ birthday.

You have always understood something so vital about aging — keep learning, find ways to volunteer, contribute and build community around you. And you do all of this — and do it so well. We admire you, Dad, and we love you so much for always being you. You are always asked about the secret to your longevity, but your real secret is knowing what makes a good life and knowing how to lead it, day by day. You wake up each morning, put both feet on the floor and know what you're about to do and why it matters. Each day holds possibilities for learning, volunteering, doing good work in the world. You live with gratitude for each day, for the life you have been given and for the simple pleasures of a good cup of coffee and good conversation. You are a wise, great person, but your greatness is not just in the number of years lived, but in the abundance and enthusiasm with which you have chosen to live these years.

Walter indeed chose optimism over pessimism and hope over fear. Throughout his hundred years, he has looked forward and sought to make the best of the situation he has been dealt. At fifteen, he was determined to get his family out of Germany. After Kristallnacht it was Walter's dogged determination to obtain exit visas that saved his family. With only a quarter in his pocket he was able to find employment in New York City within three days of arriving in America. He fought with valor for his new country through a series of brutal island battles in World War II. He started a successful business which still carries his name today. He became a senior vice-president of a successful chain of department stores. He is a loving and devoted father of two children, four grandchildren, and four great-grandchildren. Upon his retirement, Walter embarked on a 32-year career as a volunteer in Terre Haute, his adopted American hometown. At age 95,

Walter was awarded the highest honor that can be bestowed on a civilian by Federal Republic of Germany. These events testify to Walter Sommers' accomplishments. However, they don't accurately describe his character and personality. He is and has been many things during his long life—son, brother, husband, father, uncle, grandpa, great-grandpa, and friend—much respected, much beloved.

One constant is Walter's eternal optimism. He envisions a world in which everybody treats one another with respect and kindness. He has seen the darkest side of humanity and lived to remind us how it could happen again if we don't learn from our mistakes. Walter is a light in this world. He shows us what can be done with our lives in the time we are allotted.

Walter Wins Army Artillery Award

Walter receives The Honorable Order of Saint Barbara

`Walter continues to receive honors after his 100th birthday. On April 9, 2021, Walter was presented the Honorable Order of Saint Barbara by Sgt. Lucas Worthington of the Indiana National Guard. The award is given to individuals who have demonstrated the highest standards of integrity and moral character, displayed an outstanding degree of professional competence, served the Artillery with selflessness; and contributed to the promotion of the Artillery branch.

The award came through the nomination of Major Chaplain Aaron Rozovsky, of the District of Columbia Army National Guard. When Rozovsky was a student at Hebrew Union College, he was assigned to United Hebrew Congregation in Terre Haute in 2016 and 2017. There, he met Walter and Louise and learned of their story.

"They were just the greatest couple," said Rozovsky, who is now Rabbi of Beth El Congregation in Winchester, Virginia. "It's such a blessing to hear his story because in a few years, we won't have anyone left from his generation. It's important for adults and kids to hear his testimony and about the Holocaust what he went through."

On Memorial Day 2021 the City of Terre Haute displayed a banner with Walter's image on Ohio Avenue to honor him as a Hometown Hero.

During our last interview, I asked Walter how he would like to be remembered. "That's simple," he laughed. "I want to be remembered as an ordinary man who lived a wonderful life." Walter went on to argue that this biography should be titled "An Ordinary Guy Who Did the Best that He Could."

When I told him that the title was going to be "A Reluctant Hero," he shook his head. "I'm no hero!" he protested. Those who have met Walter beg to differ.

My wife Angie and I have had the honor to interview Walter on 50 different occasions over the past of two years. During that time, Walter and Louise became very dear to us. We have also had the privilege to get to know Ron and Nancy Sommers, Josh Alper, and many other family members. It has been an honor to help Walter relive his hundred years and to be the one to write his biography.

Rick Kelsheimer   June 14, 2021

Walter and Louise with Ron Sommers and Family

Walter and Louise with Nancy Sommers and Family

Epilogue

In the process of writing this book I came across a autobiography Louise had written in 1941. It was her first-hand recount of her early life and the events that brought her to America. Louise was sixteen at the time and had an amazing command of the English language. She was optimistic with her life before her. I felt that it was too important and precious not to include in the book.

Looking Back
By Louise C. Levite

To my warmly loved friend Gertrude Pelz
To Whom I would have liked to tell this tale.

Chapter I

Not even the greatest genius can remember the days when he was still in his diapers, and neither can I.

The first time I remember being myself when I was supposed to have my picture taken, a thing which I hated and still do, so I always stuck my tongue out or started crying and you can see how the pictures turned out.

I remember learning to swim when I was about four years old. Everyone admired me and I naturally tried to show off. I wanted to dive in from a high springboard, but I fell flat on my stomach. If you ever had this experience, then I think you will sympathize with me. I only know that I have never tried it since – and I don't think I will ever again.

I remember being awakened one morning by my governess and being told to dress quickly and come into my parents room. There I found in a cradle, a red little thing and I was informed that this was my sister. I remember remarking how little she was. I must have tried to take her tiny fingers, when she started crying and I was quickly taken out of the room.

Chapter II

At the age of five, I had diphtheria which kept me in bed for a long time. Afterwards my parents took me to the mountains to get my strength back. I remember being at a café there, wearing my fathers' hat and stopping at every table taking the hat off and saying: "Hello, how are you?"

The next thing that comes to my mind is the time my uncle came from America. He usually came every two years and brought us beautiful presents. I remember that he asked me if I would like to come to America. My answer was: "Yes when I'm a big girl." *Another thing that stands out from that visit is that he promised both my cousin and me each a car when we shall reach the age of eighteen. When I reminded him of this last year he said a promise is a promise and he won't forget. I hope that he will still be of the same opinion when we are eighteen years!

Next I remember the time my cousin, who is ½ year older than I, was visiting us. At that time I was very energetic and exercised every morning. My cousin who was rather lazy never liked to join me. One day I wanted to show off and I kicked my foot so high in the air that I fell backwards. My pain wouldn't stop, so they went to have me x-rayed. The doctor who was very unfriendly, told me not to make such a fuss about it. It would hurt me for another three weeks but would be O.K. then. This was 1930 and the doctor was a Nazi already.

Chapter III

We have now approached the historic day: April 16, 1931. At least for me it is historic, for this was the day that I proudly marched to school for the first time in my life. I was not quite six and therefore the youngest in the class of 1A.

In front of the school, I met my two best friends, Trude and Gretel, each on the hand of their mother also. Our mothers had gone to school together too, and now we were repeating it all over again.

Ascending the stairs the smiles slowly faded from the faces of the three little girls and they held their mothers hands a little tighter. I don't remember exactly what happened, but I think we had recess at ten and the mothers left then. One little girl started screaming and yelling when she noticed that her mother was leaving, so the poor teacher could do nothing but let her stay.

I can't recall what happened on that first day in school, but I know that I had my picture taken afterwards wearing a black apron over my new dress, a satchel on my back and a "Schultüte" in each arm. In Germany it is a custom to give children a "Schultüte" when they start school. It is cone shaped and out of cardboard and the outside is covered with colored paper. It is usually filled with candies, cookies, fruit and other presents (at least mine were).

I don't think that anything outstanding happened in my first year of school. I know that my first report card was very good and my grandfather gave me a dime for every 1 (like A here) a nickel for every 2 (like B here) and I had to give him a nickel for every 3 (C), 4(D) or 5 (F). Thank goodness I never got anything lower than 2 in all my schooldays in Germany, excepting Art and Music in which I usually got 3.

Chapter IV

The day after my 7th birthday my mother suddenly died. Since then things have never been the same. My sister was only 2½ years at the time and so of course she can't remember anything. Although I was already seven I must confess that I hardly remember anything about it.

I know that my whole family came and my aunts stayed with us for a year and were almost like a real mother to us. After that we had always a governess, whom I didn't particularly care for.

Soon after my mother died my grandfather died also. It seems that with my mother's death a chain of misfortunes started. Hitler came to power and my uncle was beaten up, put into prison by Nazis and later had to flee to France. Another aunt and uncle and children left for England, which was lucky in a way. My best friend's father was <u>murdered</u> by the Nazis. Jewish stores were boycotted, and of course my fathers was one of them.

In 1935 or 6 there was a law passed that Jewish people were not allowed to have a Christian maid that was not over 45 years of age. And so our maid whom we liked so much had to leave us and instead we had to take an old woman who hardly did any work, but whom we dare not offend. I won't bother you with the many horrible stories I know, for we hear enough and read enough terrible things as it is.

Chapter VI

Ouch! I pinched myself again and again to see that it was not a dream. Ouch! It must be true!—I really was on my way to London. I could hardly sit still. I was so excited. I was eleven at the time and this was to be my first visit to London and all by myself at that. Well, practically. Of course there was a lady, a friend of my aunt's, who was to look after me, but I didn't even know her.

Well, here I was on the Express, feeling very important and envied by all my friends for none of them had ever been to London before. Comfortably sitting in the sleeping compartment at last, I found that I had a beautiful American lady sharing it with me. She offered me some candy and I tried to show her that I knew a little English but instead of "Thank you very much" I said, "Please very much". When she started to laugh I realized my mistake and I am pretty sure I shall never make it again.

At six o'clock we were awakened by the conductor and told that we were now at the Belgian Frontier. He examined our passports and asked us if we were taking any money out of Germany. In Ostende, just before crossing the channel we had our baggage examined. This was the first time that I had been on a boat and did I get seasick! I shall leave my feelings up to your imagination. One thing I shall tell you however – I had to change my dress twice. Of course I was only too happy to land in Dover. After 1½ hours from there the train slowly rolled into Victoria Station and I saw my aunt after three years of separation again.

I stayed in London for the whole summer vacation, and I had a wonderful time. Only three sad things occurred while I was there and they were: 1st I lost a golden necklace, 2nd I forgot to take my watch off before going swimming and 3rd I gained 15 lbs. But on the whole, I really had a grand time. and I was only too sorry to go back to Germany and school.

But it was only a year before I was to make that journey again.

Chapter VII

My last days in Germany were very exciting for we did not want anyone to know that we were leaving and had to get everything ready for our departure. My grandmother, uncle, aunt, and cousin had left a week before us already.

I remember on the last day I was just walking to the post office when I met a schoolfriend of mine who wanted to borrow a book from me. I told her to get it the next day, but she insisted that she would like to have it right away. Not wishing her to get suspicious or to hurt her feelings I told her to come along. When the maid saw us, she quickly slammed the door in our faces and carried the suitcases and the trunks that were standing in the hall in my father's bedroom. Excusing herself she opened the door again and told us that there was such a mess in the hall that she didn't like for us to come in. P.S. I don't think that my friend believed her, but that doesn't matter today. I only knew that I got a scolding for bringing her with me.

At last the time had come! 2:30 P.M., September 26, 1937, and the train was slowly pulling out of the small little station and with tear-stained eyes I saw the houses of Straubing pass by for the last time. We had not even said goodbye to my grandparents to spare them and us all the excitement and grief. I was not sad for long, for was I not fortunate to get out of Germany!

In London there was a happy reunion of the family. But a week later there were tears on everyone's faces again for my grandmother, two aunts, two uncles and my cousin were leaving for America on the "Queen Mary". My father was returning to Germany, and we were staying in England with my aunt and uncle, until my father had wound up his business and would then get us and take us to America. Our only consolation: "We'll all see each other in America soon!"

Chapter VIII

My sister and I stayed in England for exactly ½ year. We could not go to a public school there since my father did not pay taxes and so we had to attend private school. There I really lost ½ year of school, because I was with girls much younger and the only thing I learned was the language. I was always the best in Arithmetic for I could figure that out in German and numbers are numbers in any language.

On Christmas my father visited us and he never returned to Germany. He went to Switzerland instead and waited for the visa to America there. You see at that time everything was easy compared to now. On the 23rd of March we sailed from Plymouth aboard the "Normandie".

We had a swell time on board, for we were hardly seasick. We went to the movie every day, went swimming, saw Punch and Judy shows, played ping pong and did many other exciting things. We had a very important passenger aboard – his name – President Hoover. I am still angry that I didn't get his autograph.

You can't imagine how I felt when I first saw the Statue of Liberty and the skyscrapers of New York in the background. I think it sort of says: "Welcome, stranger."

I stayed in New York for ten days and then I went to Terre Haute, Indiana, where I lived for the next 2 ¼ year.

Chapter IX

I celebrated my thirteenth birthday in my new home in my new country April 24th 1938. There was not only fun to think of, however, for after a few days I had to take a sort of examination from the principal of all the schools. I was much too nervous to have my senses all together. Since I had not the slightest idea of American history or geography, I was put in 6A. Since I knew arithmetic of 6B – and 6A and 6B were in one room and were taught by one teacher anyway – I was soon put in 6B.

I took the 7A work in summer school and in September I was put in 7B2. But I was not satisfied with that, and I told the principal that I would like to be in 7B1 (there were no rapids). The reason why I had not been put in 7B1 is that in summer school there was no Latin taught. The principal told me if I would be willing to make up the half year that I missed, he would be glad to put me in 7B1, which I did.

I'm not in my right class now, though, for when I first came I should have been put in 7B, but I can't help that now.

I liked it very much in Terre Haute. We had our own little house. Everyone knew everyone else and everybody else's business of course, which was not so pleasant in a way.

On Sundays we went to the Club where we could ride a pony, play tennis, ping pong, or golf none of which I ever did and for which I could still kick myself. The only other amusement were of course the movies or picnicks. There is one advantage that New York has over small towns. One has a better opportunity and chance to do different things.

Chapter X

I must say that I liked it in Terre Haute very much and I thought that I would never like New York. But I have changed my mind – it will soon be a year that I am here. I have many friends now, some of them still from Europe but many of them true Americans.

I used to think, that I can't get used to the noise and the traffic, the hurry and the excitement, the pushing and the running, but now I love it and I think I would miss it very much if we should move. I used to think that your own private house and a garden in front and back were the only thing that I would care for. Although I still prefer it, I don't think that I dislike living in an apartment at all.

I liked the Joan of Arc Jr. High School right from the start. It was so modern and new, and I was not the only stranger there. Although I think that a lot of the girls were stuck up, even though I never saw any reason to be stuck up about, I liked it there on the whole very much.

Since February 1941 I go to Julia Richman High School, which I truly think to be a very fine school.

My aim for the near future is: to lose my accent, not to be so bashful and to land on every Honor Roll of Julia Richman.

The End

Tributes and Thoughts
about Walter

Walter Sommers is a living breathing encyclopedia of history and I feel fortunate to call him my friend.

Eva Moses Kor

No greater example of inspired living exists in any community than Terre Haute's Walter Sommers. The man witnessed the Kristallnacht at the brink of the Holocaust, escaped Nazi Germany with his family and saw combat with the U.S. Army during World War II. Nearly a dozen of Walter's extended family died, along with millions of other Jewish people, from Nazi atrocities. Yet, he's lived on, rooted in an eternal optimism. He chose hope over fear.

Once he retired, Walter continued to volunteer with several local causes – the public library, Red Cross, hospice, and Terre Haute's CANDLES Holocaust museum. "Giving to others, helping others – to me, that was important," he told me, days before turning 100 years old. Thousands of people in this city would say, "I want to be like Walter when I grow up."

Mark Bennett
Terre Haute Tribune Star

Walter is a man who has touched so many lives during his lifetime.

Mike Tank   WTWO NBC News

Walter Sommers is a survivor, historian and docent, and friend. He is a real treasure to me but to the entire staff of the CANDLES Holocaust Museum and Education Center.

Walter is gracious enough to share his story with the museum; although Walter does not consider himself a Holocaust survivor, he is. His family's business was destroyed, and his father was imprisoned at Buchenwald Concentration Camp during Kristallnacht. With great prodding from Walter early on, the Sommers family applied for visas to immigrate to the United States. Shortly after Walter's father was imprisoned, the visas came through and the family was able to get their father out of the camp and safely leave the country with their possessions, but without any money. The Sommers' story adds a new perspective to the main exhibit at CANDLES, allowing people to gather a variety of perspectives.

Walter is a lifelong learner and reader, but most importantly a teacher. He loves to sit with visitors and discuss the why of the Holocaust. He thinks it is imperative for the visitor to understand the end of World War I and the Treaty of Versailles and he begins his story here. With some prompting, he also adds in his personal experiences. Statistically speaking, learning from a survivor is one of the best ways to retain information but also become much more compassionate about human rights issues. We are thankful that Walter so willingly gives his time to the museum.

When I began at CANDLES, I made it a point to visit with Walter regularly. The conversations remained professional as he was trying to teach me too; but I surprised him with my knowledge of history and the Holocaust. Our chats quickly turned to the topic of books that we have each read and suggestions for each other, cementing our friendship. After almost four years, I have been assigned as an essential family caregiver and have been able to visit with Walter at his home during the pandemic. These visits still inspire me and continue to make me smile. He always asks how the museum is doing and then shares some precious nugget of information with me. Our friendship has become a highlight of my time at CANDLES and I look forward to seeing Walter.

Leah Simpson: Director CANDLES Holocaust Museum and Education Center

"I have a question...!"

Looking back on the many encounters with Walter, it occurs to me that almost every conversation, every letter, every email comes to the point that he asks: "I have a question ...!" This question expresses Walter's tremendous curiosity, with which he seeks to understand political and historical events of the past and the present – and in particular, he follows events in Europe and Germany with keen interest.

Walter Sommers has lived in Terre Haute/Indiana for many years, but he was born and raised in Frankfurt, the place where I was born and where I live today. Because of his Jewish origin Walter had to leave Germany with his family in 1939.

How did I meet Walter and Louise Sommers? It has to do with the great commitment of the city of Frankfurt, which since 1980 has invited former citizens who had to flee Germany during the Nazi period to visit their former hometown again. Around the same time, I initiated the Project Jewish Life in Frankfurt, in which a group of volunteers accompanies the guests of the city, researches for them and invites them to talk to young people in schools.

So in 1989 I met Walter's cousin Max Sommers and his wife Ruth – and visited them several times in Dayton, Ohio. When Max and Ruth reported on their experiences in Frankfurt, Walter became curious. For many years he wanted nothing more to do with Germany. On the one of my visits to Dayton, Walter and Louise set out to meet me there – and decided in 1992 to follow the invitation of the city of Frankfurt.

Walter gladly accepted the offer of the Project, to get in touch with students. It was particularly important to him to attend his former school, the Musterschule, about which he always reports with shining eyes. He also spoke in the Schule am Ried, where I was teaching at that time, about his own experiences and the history of his family.

Such conversations with contemporary witnesses are of great importance since they give a name and a human face to those who have been discriminated against and persecuted. In this way, empathy can arise. Life stories are an important basis for a better understanding of historical events and their consequences for those affected and thus counteract anti-Jewish stereotypes. And conversely, it is important for former Frankfurters like Walter to be heard in the country from which they were expelled. The interest of young people in Germany in the life stories and fates of the persecuted is a hopeful sign, that helps Walter to feel reconnect with his birthplace.

In the same year Nancy came with her two daughters Rachel and Alex to follow in the footsteps of her parents and grandparents in Frankfurt and Straubing.

Since then we have been in close contact, by letter, by mail, with calls, with my visits to Terre Haute and Boston – and more recently with zoom meetings. We exchange ideas about God and the world. Walter shares his memories with me, I contribute results from archive research.

With the entry into retirement age, Walter strengthened his admirable and varied voluntary commitment. He is active as a contemporary witness in schools and universities and is still lecturing in the Candles Museum in Terre Haute/Indiana, founded by Eva Kor.

Since 2012, the city invites the following generations every year to visit the former home country of the parents, as the only city in Germany. The two children of Louise and Walter Sommers, Ron with his wife Charles Mary Kubrick and Nancy with her partner Josh Alper, also came to Frankfurt in 2012 and 2013.

Walter loved the Taunus Mountains. When Ron got the invitation of the city of Frankfurt, the wires ran hot. Walter Sommers gave his son recommendations on what to see or explore there: the Musterschule that Walter once attended, the apartments in Loenstraße and Finkenhofstraße, the headquarters of the Wittwe-Hassan store chain in Hanauer Landstraße, which his grandfather had built, etc. And Walter gave me on the way to remind Ron that he should take his hiking boots with him, because we were supposed to explore the Taunus mountains together and to walk to the Fuchstanz, where the hiking tours of the Sommers often led on the weekends.

When Nancy returned to Frankfurt one year later, she took part in the laying of two stumbling blocks for Ernst and Margot Sommer. Uncle Ernst always had impressed little Walter when he spoke proudly about his experiences in the First World War. The fact that he, who had risked his life for Germany in the war, was later deported and murdered, is particularly painful.

Both, Ron and Nancy, gave a final speech in the Frankfurter Römer, the historical townhall, on behalf of the group of visitors at the end of their one week stay and emphasized the importance of the visit to their parents' former homeland for them. These visits brought the history of their ancestors in Germany closer to them – and back to the memory of the family.

I am glad, that I was able to contribute to the Sommer family being present and visible in Frankfurt again, with articles about the history of the family in books and on the website of the Project Jewish Life in Frankfurt, with a film portrait about Walter's cousin Marthel, with stumbling blocks reminiscent of Uncle Ernst and his daughter Margot and of Max and Marthel's parents Salomon and Betty Sommer.

Despite of his advanced age Walter Sommers continues to be intensively involved with Jewish history, conveying both his own life story and general information about the history of Germany, with which he wants to contribute to an appropriate and differentiated image of Germany in the United States.

Conveying the history of the Jews in Germany and in Europe has become for him a life task. For this he was honored in 2016 with the Federal Cross of Merit, an honor that initially irritated him a little, but then filled him with pride.

It is important for Walter to be in touch with his birthplace and with Germany again. I am happy to be the bridge to his former homeland. It was a special pleasure for Walter that the Musterschule brought him warm congratulations on his 100th birthday with a short film.

Walter's life story exemplifies what it means to be discriminated against and persecuted, to have to leave the homeland and all that was built there. On the one hand, his life shows how difficult the new beginning was, but also impressively how powerful the emigrants have developed in managing and shaping their new life. It is admirable how Walter is involved not only within the family, but also in his environment by making a contribution to a better world on the basis of his own experiences.

It is wonderful that Walter's story and that of his family are being re-membered and made known in many ways to the general public in Ger-many and in his present homeland, including this book. May it find many inquisitive readers.

Angelika Rieber Frankfort, Germany
Family friend, family historian, Chairwoman of Project Jewish Life in Frankfurt

In the winter of 1995, my husband and I were greeted to the city of Terre Haute with a thick sheet of snow. Along with what little money we had, we brought along our dreams of pursuing a master's degree in the country that Korea looked up to. Although most of our salary post-undergrad had gone into saving up for that moment, it became apparent that it couldn't support both of our education after we put down the advance for the apart-ment. While scraping whatever money we could before the next semester began, my husband asked ISU if I could at least receive the free English tutoring from the school library that he was receiving before the following semester. The school denied his request, stating that they couldn't accept non-students for student-only programs. However, they did refer him to another free English program in the Vigo County Library just a couple blocks south of campus. I went to the library, and they assigned me a tutor: Mr. Sommers.

I became Mr. Sommers' second student in the spring of 1996. His les-sons on Thursday were not restricted to books or the Vigo Country Library. We would go to the local marts and he introduced me to what Americans bought and ate. He invited me to his home and showed me what life in the American suburbia was like. For him, the lessons in ink were only as good as their applications in the world. I have fond memories of him taking me to the Candles Holocaust Museum and Education Center, where he also volunteered as an educator. While the Candles Museum wasn't a large establishment at the time, his passion for his work there made its collection rich. Mr. Sommers told me that he valued the memory of humanity's past in the collective memory of the future generation, emphasizing that we are here today because of where we were yesterday.

As a young foreign couple studying in the United States, trivial matters were sometimes difficult to deal with fluency. Around Christmas after finals, my husband and I headed to Chicago to celebrate our third wedding anniversary. After two hours of driving across the state, somewhere in between Chicago and Terre Haute, our tiny red car stopped on the road. My husband efforts to fix the car started again were to no avail. The transmission was broken and needed to be replaced. With no cellphone and distressed in a foreign environment, we resorted to calling the one American phone number that we knew: Mr. Sommer's home line. In search of a phone, we started walking up to what few houses were in our vicinity. However, the scarcely populated town, if we could even call it a town, was not keen on letting strangers into their homes. Several rejections and one kind lady later, we got a hold of a phone and called Mr. Sommers. When my husband told him the news, Mr. Sommers quickly referred us to an honest local mechanic who could fix our car back to Terre Haute. After the call, he sent a tow truck for us, in his own expense, to fetch us and our car back to Terre Haute.

This was not the first time that Mr. Sommers saved one of his tutees from their capsized vehicle in the middle of rural America's vast nothingness. A Chinese student of his was in a car accident. Fortunately, he was not hurt but the door of the driver's seat had to be replaced. After bringing his tutee back to Terre Haute, Mr. Sommers advised him to find a replacement door at a junkyard instead of paying full price for a new door. The student was apparently on a budget, so he took Mr. Sommers' advice and headed to the junkyard. Fortunately, he did find a door that could fit his car. Unfortunately, he got a red door for his blue car.

While these stories of Mr. Sommers helping his students fix their cars may seem trivial, I am grateful that he was always there for us both in and out of class. Living in a foreign country sometimes comes with bigger difficulties than missing Korean food. Perhaps the problems seemed bigger than they were because everything seemed different and new in America. It was never Mr. Sommers' burden to help his students after hours. Nevertheless, he was always there for us and others both in and out of class, always selfless yet never unsparing. His guidance helped us recalibrate ourselves during disorienting situations, but acknowledged of our capacity to move forward under our own provision.

After graduating, my husband and I moved back to South Korea to pursue our careers. The distance between Seoul and Terre Haute was felt much shorter than it actually was with the advent of the Internet. Mr. Sommers and I would send each other regular updates and holiday greetings. As per the fad of the time, his warm greetings were always accompanied with brightly colored animations gilding the frieze of the email.

It wouldn't be until 2002 that I would see Mr. Sommers in person again. My husband and I thought that this would be a great time to see him again and for our 36-month old son to meet him for the first time. Mr. Sommers graciously allowed my son and I to stay in his home for the week that we visited Terre Haute. During this short yet meaningful week, I got to see how Mr. Sommers kept himself busy on a daily basis. With the break of dawn, he would get out of bed and head first to the garden. After taking care of some gardening work, he would sit down and read the local paper and the New York Times after fixing a quick breakfast. His mornings would either be split doing volunteer work or small chores. I recall one morning when we went to the supermarket together. After dropping my son off at the daycare center near his home, he gathered coupons that he had cut out from the local papers previously. Nothing of excess was accounted for, only taking with him the coupons for items that were essential. Before leaving, he calculated an approximate course and time. He took into account each movement and stop by the minute, trying to maximizing things that got done and minimized wasted time. During the grocery run, he stopped by two stores; buying the most economic option on his list from each. He stopped for gas on the way back, making sure he had a full tank the next time he was out.

A couple days before leaving America for home, Mr. Sommers offered to take me to a book fair that carried an assortment of books all under a dollar. With the price of English books being exponentially more expensive back home, I bought enough Children's books for my son to fill two Tupperware crates. Seeing me carry the two boxes of dollar books, Mr. Sommers joked, "this boy will one day teach you English".

And maybe he was right. 16 years later, my son got accepted to NYU to study Political Science. After sending our goodbyes to him in New York, my husband and I rented a car and took a road trip to Indiana, like we did on that cold winter day 22 years ago. When we arrived near Mr. Sommers' new residence in Westminster Village, a retirement community in Terre Haute, he instantly stood out from the rest of the folks on the communal porch. Lined with sunbeds facing the driveway, most of them were relaxing, some of them were talking to each other, few were silent, but only Mr. Sommers was hunching forward towards today's issue of the New York Times in his hands.

Nearly approaching a century at the time, we honestly expected him to take things a little slower by then. However, he didn't cease to surprise us with his tireless itinerary. He was scheduled to talk at the Candles Holocaust Museum, the same institution he volunteered when I first met him, at 2PM. Although now time and age weakened his legs, it hadn't dwindled his fascination. He spoke with greater insight than when I first heard him so many years ago.

Seeing him address the people with the same passion that he demonstrated to me three decades ago, I couldn't help but wonder if all those years had even slightly changed Mr. Sommers. I recalled him telling me to 'keep yourself busy' throughout the years. Perhaps this was how he stayed sharper than ever with every year. It wasn't that his dedication stayed firmly anchored to his love for this life, but rather, paddled constantly to avoid fading into the currents of time. We only met once a week for an hour during my time at ISU, he committed more than that into teaching me English. While superficially he was teaching me English, it was more than that for me. Language was about more than communicating thoughts; but also values and emotions that wove the intimate fabric of human connection. For these lessons, I thank him from the bottom of my heart. I have and will cherish the values that he demonstrated though his actions. But above all,

I will always be grateful for the love and wisdom he so kindly shared to a stranger that happened to stumble across his life.

Now it's your turn. Would you introduce yourself?" His voice softly pulsated through the quiet air of the Vigo County Library.

I said something about myself to my new tutor, Mr. Sommers. But he said, "I can't hear you, Myousun. Can you speak up? Look at me in the eyes." My words were hindered by my timid personality, waning as they exit my thoughts. This was the first time I was learning English one-on-one with a teacher. Coming from a Confucian background, we were taught that 'a student shouldn't even step on a teacher's shadow'. Students should listen and not talk-over the teacher. That was the etiquette that was expected of us. Society's projection of teachers made them more difficult than they were. The hierarchical strata diving the teachers and the students was always apparent—and always looming around in the classroom.

I tried to speak up with a reddish face, but my new tutor was still asking me to speak up more. Several months later, Mr. Sommers stopped asking me to speak up. He raised my voice. He gave me the confidence to look someone in the eye when I talked with others. While this may seem trivial, this is fundamental to basic conversation; an honest expression of self. That is a way of showing 'I can do it.' The tutorial session with Mr. Sommers lasted for 2 years during my graduate studies.

Last night, while perusing through Mr. Sommers' teaching materials after several decades, tears of deep thankfulness dropped. He prepared a lot of things to teach just one student with pleasure, without even being paid. He volunteered to help poor strangers in his community. The classes were never just spent time talking with his student. He never missed bringing teaching materials for his student that he typed himself, something for reading from the newspapers or books and homework. I had to do homework. He corrected errors of my writing or speaking.

Anyone who had experience of volunteering knows even one hour once a week was not easy. Mr. Sommers went well beyond and devoted not only his time but his heart into teaching a stranger. That is affection to strangers. He cared for people regardless of their cultural background.

Years later I had some students who were shy and had difficulty in looking into my eyes during my English class in Korea. I found myself saying the same thing to my students as Mr. Sommers did to me. The result is their changes that I experienced long ago.

His tutoring was not just at the library.

Myosun Kim, Seoul, Korea

Granddad always amazes me with his utter modesty, even his nonchalance, about the vast world of experiences he has inside him. There's basically nothing this man hasn't seen and yet there's never a touch of aggrandizement in the way that he speaks. He remains so warm and loving—and above all practical!

Devin Fore, Walter's Grandson

The thing that I know well about my grandpa is that his spirit and energy is contagious. He has a way of inspiring and uplifting everyone around him and it's a real gift. He cares for others deeply – his family, his English students, his community – and he never loses focus of the things that matter to him. I've never heard him say anything petty or unloving – which I've taken for granted my whole life I think, but I now understand how remarkable it is to get to 100 years and be able to uplift others around you naturally and with ease.

One story we laugh about 25+ years later is the time he stomped on my hamster when I was a kid, thinking he was protecting my grandma from a rat after she shrieked. He felt so guilty, but we all understood it was a mistake and now many years later I still hear him tell the story often since it was so memorable and such a classic blunder. You might be thinking that's not a very nice memory, but here's what I think: I love that he can simultaneously be apologetic but also understand that in the scheme of life, that's a pretty minor mistake and our relationship can easily withstand something like that. He knows that life is fragile, and because of that, we have to laugh and keep loving each other.

Alex Hays, Walter's granddaughter

My Uncle Walter is an inspiration to so many! Walter has strong and well-defined views of racial and social justice. He has been a role model to me and my family because he put his beliefs into action throughout his life. He provided direct support and mentorship to so many in his community. He educated generations about the holocaust in an effort to deter similar atrocities in the future. He tutored immigrants struggling to learn English ensuring that they too would have opportunities for success in the United States. He worked to ensure equal rights and opportunities for his co-workers in the department store and challenged the racial discrimination of the1960's. Walter Sommers' personal story is one of honor, respect and resilience in the midst of life's challenges. Throughout the years he has focused on caring for family and friends. To reach a 100 is remarkable but to reach out and help so many is a life well lived and a man we all should aspire to emulate.

Linda Gerson, Walter's niece

It may come as a surprise to people who know Walter that he greatly enjoys riding in a pick-up truck. On visits to Nancy and me, Walter made known that if there was a choice between the car and the truck, he preferred the truck. Well into his nineties, he'd place one foot on the running board, grasp the grip above the door, and hoist himself into the passenger seat in one swift motion. Gazing around, he commented on the elevated view, and never failed to note approvingly of the manual transmission. If the ride was long enough, he might launch into a reminiscence of driving 4x4 weapons carriers or 'deuce and a half' cargo trucks down boggy jungle tracks on Guam or in the Philippines during World War II. Or we'd compare his experience as a Wandervogel bicycling in pre-war Germany to mine on a six-week cycling trip through the Canadian Maritimes in 1965.

Our trips generally led to Costco or Stop & Shop, where Walter took charge of the shopping cart, navigating speedily down the aisles. Four decades of retail experience have given Walter a practiced eye — uniquely, he refers to the types of apples, pears, and other produce by their four-digit SKU numbers. "These 3031s look good, let's buy a half dozen."

These outings gave us an opportunity to talk between ourselves , and long after my father and uncles had passed away were a rare chance to share time with someone of an older generation.

Josh Alpers, Walter's son-in-law

When I think about Walter I think about his brave ancestors who lived on an estate and were cattle dealers in Northern Hesse Germany. His grandfather was a butcher who fought in the war of 1870/71 between Germany and France with his brother and an uncle. His father moved to Frankfurt and opened 34 thriving stores. They were Germans first and Jewish second. They were betrayed by their country in the most despicable way and forced to find a new home in the United States. When I think about Walter I think about his brave mother, grandmother, great grandmother, great-great grandmother who did the hard work of nurturing the family, raising the children and grandchildren while navigating treacherous times. They cared for and loved the family fiercely. Most of all when I think about Walter I think about his loving and strong wife, Louise, who also came from Germany and with Walter created a new legacy through their children, grandchildren and great grandchildren.

Charles Mary Kubricht, Walter's Daughter-in-law

When I think of Grandfather the word that summarizes his life, and approach to it, is "dedication." There are many examples of this.

Firstly, he has demonstrated dedication to the United States of America through his military service. To have immigrated to this country from Germany and then quickly enlist in the US Army is beyond selfless. There is no more dedication than to be willing to die for a cause you strongly believe in.

Secondly, Grandfather had a very strong work ethic. His dedication to his career is to be admired. He believed that working hard wasn't the only key to success. Integrity, honesty and honor are what can truly make a difference.

Thirdly, Grandfather is dedicated to his faith. Judaism, and its history, are a core part of Walter. His continued desire to educate the public by volunteering at Candles Holocaust Museum is such a community asset.

His dedication to sharing his knowledge and stories is greatly important and relevant.

Demian Fore, Walter's Grandson

This is less a story than it is a story about stories, and what they mean to my grandfather: he uses his stories as a bridge to connect him with others. There's a Jewish saying, there is nothing so whole as a broken heart. The idea is that heartbreak connects us to a wider community when we can understand our pain as a source of commonality, shared humanity, through our frailties and fears, our loss and longing. Walter could have boarded up his heart like a shattered glass window after Kristallnacht, the night of broken glass. Instead he has always used his stories as a bridge connecting his experience with others. He extends a story like an outstretched hand in greeting, an invitation to connect across continents and generations.

My 4-year-old son Oren has never wanted a haircut, and has long flowing golden hair extending the full length of his back. Rather than see Oren's resistance to haircuts as a dilemma to be solved, or a problem requiring intervention, Walter told Oren the story of how he was once a long-haired boy in Frankfurt, who had never had his hair cut until at age 4 he ran away from home to the barber and on his own asked for, and received, his first haircut.

Walter uses his stories to make people feel welcome with him, understood by him, embraced by him. There is no difference in experience that Walter doesn't bridge through story. He has chosen, over and over, to use his experience, his life, as a source of connection—his inquisitive delight in the particularities of mundane life, the tremendous love he has shared with family and his beloved wife Louise, his suffering in Nazi Germany, his courage in building a new life in America. And through connecting his stories with others, Walter's stories and strength live in so many of us and have become ways that we too understand our own lives and loves, fears and sorrows.

Rachel Chunnha, Walter's Granddaughter

Growing up in a suburb outside NYC, it was always exciting when my aunt, uncle and cousins from Terre Haute came to visit. Even as a young child, I recall what a wonderful storyteller Uncle Walter was. Whether it was a tale about that day's work in the market buying coats for the Meis Brothers' store(s) or daily life in Terre Haute, his stories opened up new worlds to me. Walter always impressed me as friendly and outgoing. Since those qualities struck me as unusual, I attributed them (probably mistakenly) to Walter becoming a Midwesterner and a Hoosier, and thus seemed different from family members who settled in and around NYC.

Once while I was already teaching at Rutgers, Walter came to the New Jersey campus with other sales staff to watch Larry Bird play. Some months later, he told a story about his trip to watch this important basketball game. I believe I protested or at least teased him about not even calling his niece. In retrospect I take it as one more sign that Walter was steadfast in his loyalty to Terre Haute and to Indiana. Among the many traits I admire in Walter is his determined optimism. In my mind, he has learned to accept sadness and tragedy, while also recognizing it's important to move forward. It goes without saying that Walter expressed his profound grief when Louise died and yet was also able to remind himself that he needed to accept her passing. It is a way of being I'd encountered in him several times over the years. Perhaps, the earliest example of this delicate balance he strives to achieve is the story he told of their dog, Honey who died accidentally one night while on a walk with Walter. Lastly I'll add that for years, Walter has been the source of sage advice about retirement. Not only is he an exemplary retiree but has also urged me that when I retire, I need to retire to something.

Judy Gerson Walter's Niece

A Note From the Author

I consider it a privilege to document the life of such a special man. Walter Sommers has done a lot of different things during his 100 years on this planet. The most important one in my opinion is that he spent many of those years serving as a role model. By looking at Walter's life, we have been given a blueprint on how to live the life of a good human being. His motto of doing the best that you can with what you've been given has served him well. Walter has always tried to do the right thing and over the last century he has tallied a number of chits in the plus column. The world is better place because of him.

I could not have completed this book without the help of others. I would like to thank Steve Fear, Mike Brooks, Becky Nidey, Anna Schoteldraaijer, and Erik Schoteldraaijer for all of your selfless work on this project. I want to especially thank Ron and Nancy Sommers and the entire Sommers family for opening up your lives and invaluable support during the writing of this book. And of course, I need to thank my wife, Angela Kelsheimer, who spent countless hours working beside me on this endeavor.

Finally, I would like to thank Walter Sommers for sharing your life story with me. I've enjoyed every one of our minutes together and Angie and I consider you as a cherished friend.

Rick Kelsheimer